The
DUTTONS
CAN PLAY

A Boyhood Memoir of Breaking Stuff

BLAKE W. MURRI

MEDIA.COM

Published by
Illumify Media Global
www.IllumifyMedia.com
"Let's bring your book to life!"

Library of Congress Control Number: 2022913025

Paperback ISBN: 978-1-955043-86-1

Cover design by Debbie Lewis

Printed in the United States of America

Dedication

This book is dedicated to Joe, Terry, and Eddie, who are always welcome on my team.

CONTENTS

CHAPTER 1

INTRODUCTION

These are the memoirs of my childhood years, from an early age of deductive reasoning to the start of high school. I consider those my most formative years.

Some might argue that our formative years extend into high school, but for most guys (myself included), I believe deductive reasoning takes an extended hiatus about the time we enter high school. At that point, we are too preoccupied with girls and cars to think and act logically. I'd have a hard time trying to explain or rationalize what I might have been thinking in any particular situation that occurred during my high school years. Therefore, I chose to confine these memoirs to my childhood years (through the end of junior high).

This is more than an account of my life. It's a tale of adventure, athletics, and some neighbor kids who had a big impact on my life. I'll get to the neighbor kids a little later, but I should start by introducing myself.

Call me boomer. I entered the world smack dab in the middle of the baby boom, so I'm a boomer in the generational sense. I've got plenty of gray hair to show for it, and I don't shy away from that. King Solomon wrote, "Gray hair is a crown of glory; it is gained in a righteous life" (Proverbs 16:31 ESV). I can't say that I've lived an entirely righteous life, but I'm working on it. And I'll gladly accept a crown of glory for my efforts.

But it's a different sense of the word "boomer" that really defines me. I'm a boomer in the explosive sense.

My mom would say that everything changed for her the day I blasted onto the scene, that fateful day of my birth. One moment the room was peaceful, calm, and serene (notwithstanding all of the screaming, yelling, and commotion associated with her labor); the next moment, BOOM! There I was, this sweet little bundle of joy: cute, cuddly, and full of pent–up energy (after all, I'd been confined in a very tight space for the previous nine months). I was chomping at the umbilical cord to get out of there.

Right out of the hatch I was a hyperactive, energetic, busy little kid, ready for action. Mom said that I rarely slept through the night, perhaps afraid that I would miss out on something.

That persisted throughout my childhood. I dreaded having to go to bed at night. Each and every day was action packed. I couldn't rest until I had expended every last ounce of energy that I had.

Mom informed me that her only consolation in life would be for me to someday have a child of my own who was just like me. I knew that she loved me, but that sounded like the kind of love only a mother could have for her child. What, was she really wishing me on myself?

I never fully understood what Mom meant by that until I became a father and came face to face with my own little mini-me. It happened just like she wished it would. Mom lived long enough to see that. I have to give her credit for not gloating.

I eventually became a grandfather to another little mini-me. Mom didn't live long enough to see that, but I still give her credit for not haunting me in my dreams with any nightmarish gloating.

Those two mini-mes were hyperactive, energetic, busy little boys right out of the hatch. Even though they could drive me and everyone else around them crazy, I got them. I totally got them.

Though some may recoil at the thought of being labeled a boomer, I completely embrace it. That *is* my generation. Born in the mid-fifties, I lived most of my formative years in the sixties. In my humble opinion, that was the greatest time *ever* to be a kid in Small Town, USA.

Kids in my generation grew up with countless modern home conveniences that many in our parents' generation did not have, such as indoor plumbing, private phone lines, refrigerators, washers, dryers, televisions, and a myriad of other electric appliances (microwave ovens and home computers would come later). Most Americans today could not imagine life without those luxuries.

Through the wonders of modern medicine, we were protected against most serious childhood diseases, including smallpox and polio (the polio vaccine was a recent development, with mass inoculations beginning in the mid-fifties).

We enjoyed the birth of rock and roll music, and saw the Beatles perform on *The Ed Sullivan Show*. We also enjoyed the best years of rock and roll music ever to hit the air waves (again, in my humble opinion).

We witnessed the beginning of the space age, and watched with rapt attention as Neil Armstrong stepped out of the lunar landing module and took that giant leap for mankind onto the surface of the moon.

For all that was good with my generation, I have to acknowledge the bad and the ugly. In many aspects, our nation was in turmoil. Though I was just a kid during most of it, the older half of my generation was right in the thick of it.

The civil rights movement was gaining momentum, and there were epic struggles over school segregation and civil rights. The Vietnam War was in full swing, and there were anti-war protests on college campuses across the nation. The free love and psychedelic drug movements were sweeping across the country, and it was causing an upheaval in our moral fiber. These events changed our nation, some for the better, some for the worse.

Regardless of the turmoil unfolding across the country and around the world, life was fairly simple and worry free in my neck of the woods. Growing up in a small town, isolated from any visible signs of racial injustice, far removed from the big, liberal–minded college campuses, and living in a predominantly Christian community, national and international events had no immediate impact on me. I was only vaguely aware of some of those issues because we talked about them in school.

In my simple, worry–free life, I had complete freedom to play outside without adult supervision, without fear of being abducted, assaulted, or otherwise accosted. I'm sure there were a few bad actors in our community back then, but violent crime was a rare occurrence. My parents were rightfully more concerned about whatever trouble I might be causing others or bringing on myself.

BROKEN RULES

I had a good upbringing, especially in my early childhood years, with a mom and dad who both loved and cared for me. They provided me with food, clothing, and shelter, and they did everything they could to protect and prepare me for the world.

As with most families, we had rules to protect us and keep us in line. Mom was the rule maker, and Dad was the rule enforcer. I was the rule breaker.

Most of Mom's rules made sense to me, rules like "don't play in the street" and "don't play with guns." Those rules were easy to follow; it was obvious that it would not go well for me if I disobeyed them. All others were just rules; rules, schmules. Those were made to be broken.

As the rule enforcer, Dad usually provided whatever discipline was necessary when rules were broken. I wish I had a dime for every time I heard Mom say "Just wait until your father gets home!" after I had allegedly broken some rule.

That was effective, though. It always managed to put the fear of Dad in me. (At that stage of life, my fear of Dad was worse than my fear of God. Dad's discipline would be immediate and very tangible. It would be a lifetime before I'd have to face the wrath of God.)

Dad was a tough enforcer. When he had to act, he meant business. There was never a doubt as to whether or not the offense in question should ever be repeated. However, for a minor offense, Dad could be lenient. In those situations, the fear of what awaited me was worse than whatever punishment, if any, was meted out.

As for me, being the rule breaker had its challenges. I knew Mom's rules were intended for my protection, but some seemed overly protective. Others just seemed a little arbitrary.

I figured Dad wouldn't come down too hard on me if I broke those arbitrary kinds of rules. He was from the old school, where "boys will be boys." I knew that he broke a lot of rules in his day. I had heard plenty of stories to that effect from his dad.

Well, the apple didn't fall far from the tree with me. But it was a fine line to walk, knowing which rules I really had to obey and which I could break.

I don't know whether I was trying to make a point to my mom or to myself, but I was hell bent on breaking rules that just didn't make any sense. In my infinite youthful wisdom, I had to discern which of those rules could be broken without earning me a whoopin' or causing me any other sort of bodily harm. It would take a number of broken rules before I fully appreciated the wisdom behind them.

Broken Windows

Along with defining the rules of the house, Mom strived to teach me right from wrong. She was an occasional churchgoer, so I suspect she looked to the Ten Commandments as her guide. Those commandments served as a guide for our founders when they were making laws to govern our cities, states, and the nation. If they were good enough for this country, they were good enough for me.

I offer the following interpretation of the Ten Commandments as I felt they applied to me as a kid (my interpretation in italics):

1. Thou shalt have no other gods before me – *"I'll say my prayers and go to church."*
2. Thou shalt not make graven images – *"How can I make a graven image if I don't even know what one looks like? Plus, I'm not much of a sculptor. In fact, I hate arts and crafts."*
3. Thou shalt honor the Sabbath and keep it holy – *"I'll go to church on Sunday, if I'm not too busy doing something else."*

4. Thou shalt not take the name of the Lord thy God in vain – *"I won't cuss, and I won't repeat any words that come out of my dad's mouth when he's mad."*

5. Honor thy father and thy mother – *"I'll obey Mom and Dad, and I won't give them any lip."*

6. Thou shalt not kill – *"I won't kill, even when I'm really mad at my brothers and sister."*

7. Though shalt not commit adultery – *"Huh? Where's my pocket dictionary?"* (For more on that, see Chapter 6).

8. Thou shalt not steal – *"I won't take my brothers' and sister's Halloween candy."*

9. Thou shalt not bear false witness – *"I won't lie. Seriously, I won't ever, ever, ever lie."*

10. Thou shalt not covet thy neighbor's property – *"I won't beg Mom and Dad for a new bicycle like my friend just got."*

At Sunday school, I learned that breaking any of these commandments was a sin. And my teacher said that all sins are equal; however, in our household that did not seem to be the case. There was *definitely* a hierarchy of sins, with one sin being worse than any of the others.

That worst of the worst sins was the sin of lying. (None of us ever killed anyone, so I'm not sure, but that may have been worse yet.) In our family, lying was the one sin to which Dad did not turn a blind eye.

My parents were pretty good at making the punishment fit the crime, except when it came to lying. For lying, the punishment seemed to be way worse than the crime.

Most of my friends who were caught lying would get their mouths washed out with soap. To me, that made a lot of sense. Getting your mouth washed out with soap should literally make your mouth clean. And wouldn't that help to keep lies and bad words from coming out?

Well, that wasn't *my* consequence for lying. *My* consequence for lying was usually a good old fashioned whoopin'. I could refuse to go to church, repeat some of the cuss words that Dad would say, steal some of my sister's Halloween candy, or beg for a new bike like my friend just got, and I wouldn't get into very much trouble. But if (more accurately, when) I was caught lying, out came the paddle.

Needless to say, I was on the receiving end of many a well–deserved whoopin' in my time, and it was most often for lying. I learned to appreciate the words attributed to Benjamin Franklin, "Honesty is the best policy."[1] But it would take a broken window and a stiff paddle to really drive that point home for me.

Broken Norms

Besides teaching me right from wrong, Mom also taught me compassion, the ability to love my neighbors just as I love myself. My Sunday school teacher said that was a new commandment, but I was already having trouble with some of the first ten.

For some, compassion may come naturally; it might even be genetic. But not for me. That trait did not come naturally, nor was it inherited. In fact, I don't believe I was born with a single, solitary compassionate gene. Being the type A, egocentric kid that I was, even thinking of others was a foreign concept to me. I was too busy thinking about myself and looking out for number one.

Whatever amount of compassion I have today would have to be considered a learned trait. I credit Mom for teaching me that. Through her patience, persistence, and mostly her personal witness, she was eventually able to break through to the cold, dark depths of my heart and ignite a spark of compassion.

As a kid, I witnessed Mom's kindness and compassion firsthand. I was the beneficiary of that on many occasions after receiving whatever discipline I probably deserved. Mom would come to my room to console me and let me know that she loved me in spite of my misbehavior.

I observed Mom's compassion when she worked to reunite the family she married into, a family that had been torn apart through challenging times in the aftermath of the great depression.

I was with Mom when she demonstrated compassion for one of the few black families in our neighborhood, giving their kids (my classmates) rides to and from school activities. That was at a time when our nation was battling over school segregation and other racial inequalities. And I listened to Mom challenge my brother and me to have compassion for some neighbor kids when no one else did.

It would take Mom's love for her neighbors, neighbors she didn't even know, to inspire my brother and me to act, to speak up and break an unjust social norm.

Chapter 2

My Hood

American businessman and philanthropist Clement Stone wrote that we are all products of our environment.[2] It's not just the people and the culture, but also our surroundings that help to shape us.

My neighborhood had a big impact on me, what I did, what I learned, and how I lived my life. Like it or not, I am a product of that environment. In a sense, getting to know my neighborhood is part of getting to know me. So I'm going to walk you through my neighborhood, the place where I grew up.

I had just finished first grade when my parents decided it was time to purchase a home and put down some roots. They had been renters their entire married lives up to that point. They couldn't afford to buy a home while Dad was pursuing his education. They didn't really want to buy when Dad got his first "professional" job in Michigan; that was too far from "home." But after Dad landed a solid, good–paying job back home in Idaho, they were ready to settle down and buy a place of their very own.

My parents had done some early house hunting and had narrowed their selection to just a few places they thought would work. They were especially interested in a house for sale in an established neighborhood on the east side of the Snake River, north of downtown Idaho Falls.

Mom and Dad had already met with the owners for a walk-through on their own (without the distraction of kids), and they'd driven around a few times to check out the neighborhood. They wanted to walk through the house one more time with us kids along to get our response before sealing the deal. Not that our approval was required. I think they just wanted to gauge whether we would be as excited about it as they were.

The following is a description of the house and the neighborhood. Some of the details provided here will factor into the storyline later on.

The property was located on a side street in a quiet, residential area. The landscaping in front included a well–kept grass lawn, several junipers, and a few lilac bushes.

The house had three bedrooms and a single bathroom, plus separate living quarters in the basement with another bedroom and bathroom. The separate living quarters could be maintained as a rental unit. In fact, it was rented out at the time of our walk-through.

On the main floor were two unique features: 1) in the dining room was a large, plate glass window from which you could see over a fence that was just beyond the backyard, and into a ballpark on the other side, and 2) off the main hallway was a central linen cabinet, with one set of doors that opened from the hallway, and another set that opened from the bathroom. With both sets of cabinet doors open, the bathroom (and anyone in it) would be fully *exposed* from the hallway.

The backyard was divided almost in half by a cement driveway that ran the length of the yard, from the garage to an alleyway at the far end. The backyard was completely enclosed by a four-foot high chain link fence. The fence had a double gate at the end of the driveway through which the homeowners and renters could drive their vehicles onto to the property. It also had a single gate on the south side that allowed for entry to and from a neighbor's backyard.

The property itself had one peculiar feature. Along the north side of the house was a narrow, four–foot wide strip of ground where the grass lawn extended from the front. That strip of ground was held in place by a retaining wall constructed of gray cinderblock. At the far west end of that strip (on the backside of the house), the retaining wall reached its highest point, eight feet above ground level. There was no fence or any other form of barricade along the top of the retaining wall, though there should have been. It was not only a safety hazard; it was a liability suit waiting to happen.

To the north of the property was a vacant lot. The lot was over-grown with weeds, and it was home to an old, dilapidated wooden shack. No one lived there. The shack was overrun with hordes of mice, bats, and other creepy crawly things. It was still partially standing.

Stacks of rotting lumber, replete with exposed rusty nails were strewn about the ground outside the shack. It should have been con-demned. There was a big, scraggy old cottonwood tree on the lot that only added to the general unkempt appearance, with its fallen twigs and branches covering the ground below.

The whole place was a mess. Neighbors had been pleading with the property owner for years to clean it up, but to no avail. The lot was a bit of an eyesore, but it was not entirely out of character with the rest of the neighborhood.

The street to the north of the vacant lot marked the boundary line for the two grade schools in the neighborhood. Kids who lived on the south side of the boundary line went to Riverside Elementary. That's where my siblings and I would go if we were to make this move. Kids who lived on the north side of the boundary line went to Whittier

Elementary. Kids from both grade schools would all end up at the same junior and senior high schools.

Just beyond the backyard was a narrow gravel alleyway. The alleyway provided access to the driveway for this house, as well as to the few other backyard driveways that existed on the block. It was only wide enough for a single car to drive through in either direction at the same time.

The alleyway didn't get much traffic. It was mostly used by local residents, the occasional lost motorist, and the even more occasional nefarious character who was driving around looking for trouble. The alleyway had no street lights. It could be dark and scary at night . . . except when there was a baseball game underway.

On the other side of the alleyway was a ten to twelve–foot high wood vertical–slat fence, painted green. This was a perimeter fence, enclosing a ballpark that was home to the Idaho Falls Angels. The Idaho Falls Angels were a Pioneer League baseball team affiliated with the California Angels. At that time, the ballpark was called Highland Park, or more commonly, Angels ballpark.

The stadium at Highland Park was typical of ballpark stadiums of that era. The grandstands had long wooden benches for seating, with solid concrete floors and stairs. And like most professional and semi-professional ball fields from that time, Angels ballpark had bright lights for night games. As a side benefit for the neighborhood, the ballpark lights provided enough lighting to make the alleyway and surrounding streets a little safer at night.

Above the fence at mid-center field was a fully enclosed scoreboard box. The scoreboard box was wood frame construction with wood slat siding. It was painted green to match the perimeter fence. An operator (usually a teenaged kid willing to work for a few bucks) would sit in the box to post scores through the course of the game.

**My siblings and me in the backyard dressed for a parade, 1966
(Scoreboard box in the background)**

In addition to Angels ballpark, Highland Park encompassed a city park that was located to the west of the stadium. The city park included a children's playground, an old log hut, a separate kid–sized baseball field, tennis courts with parking lot, a small meandering creek, and a clump of pine trees. The pine trees had been planted near the creek in the late 1920s by early Idaho Falls pioneers. In the forty-plus years since that time, those pines had grown to impressive heights.

To the south of Highland Park was Russ's Market, the local IGA (Independent Grocers Alliance) store. The butcher at Russ's Market was one of my dad's old high school buddies. His wife also worked there as a cashier. I suspect that the butcher and his wife had a little something to do with my parents' interest in the neighborhood.

The Snake River runs about a half mile west of this property. In that part of town, the river spans about 250 feet from bank to bank. The river cuts through the old town center at Broadway Street. Just upstream from there is the natural scenic waterfalls that gave the town its name.

About three-quarters of a mile upstream of the falls, there's a small uninhabited island called Keefer's Island. The only access to Keefer's Island is by boat, though some have swum and lived to tell about it.

There's a bridge about a quarter mile upstream of the island, where US highway 20 crosses over. The Johns Hole Bridge sits about twenty feet above the water when the river is running at its average level.

Just west of the Snake River is Porter Canal. Porter Canal is used to supply water for farming. The water level and flow rate are controlled by the city water department. The canal generally runs about eight to ten feet deep, but the depth can vary seasonally. Many of Idaho Fall's finest hotels are located just to the west of Porter Canal.

As for demographics, the neighborhood at that time was primarily comprised of lower to middle–income families. The racial makeup was mostly white, with a smattering of other ethnic groups. It was an older, established neighborhood, but it was beginning to be repopulated with younger families like ours. With ours being a young, white, lower mid-dle–income family, we would fit right in.

With the neighborhood description out of the way. I'll now get back to the story.

The sellers were happy to see my parents return for a second look at the property, figuring that they were getting serious about an offer. And they were right.

While my parents were negotiating with the sellers on the price and terms of the sale, my siblings and I got a tour of the property and neighborhood from the sellers' kids. The sellers' kids were much older and "wiser" than us, so my parents were happy to have them show us around.

Our tour included a quick run through the house, a walk around the ballpark, an abbreviated playtime at the Highland Park playground, a visit to Russ's Market, and a return to the property via the gravel alleyway.

Along the way, the oldest of the sellers' kids, our primary tour guide, offered a wealth of sage advice.

At the park she told us: "There are lots of fun things to do here! In the summertime, they have arts and crafts at the log hut and tennis lessons at the courts. In the winter, they hose the parking lot down to create a rink for ice skating."

At Russ's Market, we were introduced to the candy aisle: "They have just about anything you can imagine for only five or ten cents." There were way too any choices for us to make a quick decision!

On our way back home through the alleyway, our tour guide advised: "Don't walk through the alleyway alone, and never walk through at night!"

At the end of the tour, as we were walking up the drive toward the house, our tour guide provided what she believed to be the most important bit of advice she had to offer: "Whatever you do, do not play with the Duttons."

Of course, that begged the question from me, "Who are the Duttons?"

She responded, "The Duttons are a poor family who live just up the street."

"Why should we not play with the Duttons?" I asked.

After a slight hesitation, our tour guide replied simply and directly, "Just don't play with the Duttons!"

Apparently, it needed no explanation. Though we didn't understand why, that advice was firm, and it was permanently etched in our minds: "Don't play with the Duttons."

Our tour guide noted that, though the Duttons lived very close, their property was on the other side of the boundary line for the two elementary schools. They went to a different school than we would be attending. Given that, it sounded like we would probably never have anything to do with them, so it shouldn't be an issue. Little did we know!

This house and property we were considering met all of my parents' "must haves" and most of their "nice to haves." The house was well-built and maintained, large enough for a family of six, and affordable, especially with the rental unit providing a steady revenue stream.

The property was located in a nice, quiet neighborhood that was noted for its good schools. It was not far from a major hospital (which could be important for a family with four young kids). It had a grocery store just around the corner, and it was convenient to the downtown area for other shopping and personal needs.

The lilac bushes and nearby ballpark provided a few additional selling points. (The sellers had Mom at lilac bushes, and they had Dad at ballpark!)

The biggest downside was that the house had just one bathroom. That would be a challenge, but my parents figured we could eventually expand into the rental unit, if and when finances allowed. Until then, we'd just have to make it work.

As for us kids, we didn't really know what we wanted, but this place seemed to have a lot to offer: plenty of room to play, lots of places to explore, and an easy walk to Russ's Market for a great selection of candy.

We gave it a thumbs up. (Truth be told, I'm pretty sure my parents would have bought the house whether we gave it a thumbs up, down, or sideways.) My parents completed the negotiations and sealed the deal. And with that, we packed up, said our goodbyes to . . . well, to no one, and moved to the new 'hood.

So there I was, with all the knowledge and experience that could possibly be gained from a first grade education, facing yet another move.

I was ambivalent to the thought of moving, looking neither forward nor back.

I had no basis from which to look forward. We had moved around enough that I didn't expect we'd be at the next new place very long before we'd have to move again. Why waste my thoughts on hopes and dreams that I'd have little time to fulfill?

I had no reason to look back, either. Moving as often as we did, I had never experienced a sense of permanence. I had never developed ties or lasting friendships in any of our previous locations, and it was no different this time around. I had absolutely no expectations for the new place we would soon call home. I just took it in stride that we'd be moving, and that was that.

I could not have been more wrong! If I *had* come with expectations, those expectations would have been greatly exceeded with this latest move. Not only did I get attached to the new place, I got my roots firmly planted.

We lived in that house for about eight years. In the big picture, eight years is not really that long, but it was the longest we had ever stayed in one place. And in my mind, those were a very impressionable, very wonderful, very memorable eight years. That is the place I will always remember as my childhood home.

The new neighborhood was where I would grow up, go to school, and learn the facts of life (not just the birds and the bees). It was where I would find my independence and begin to explore the world around me. It was where I would play ball and start a lifelong love for sports. It was where I would make friends and discover what true friendship really meant.

And it was where I would learn the risks of breaking rules, the consequences for breaking windows, and the rewards in breaking social norms.

CHAPTER 3

MY FAM'

Desmond Tutu, the South African Anglican bishop and theologian, wrote, "You don't choose your family. They are God's gift to you, as you are to them."[3] I'm sure there were times when I didn't seem like such a wonderful gift to my parents and siblings. Still, they were stuck with me, and I with them. They helped to influence who I am. I believe I am that much better for it. Allow me to introduce you to my family.

Dad was born in 1933 in Tetonia, Idaho. His mom died when he was quite young. His dad, my Grandpa Murri, worked for the railroad company, building the rail system across eastern Idaho and Montana. With his work on the railroad, Grandpa had to travel out of state for months at a time. The nation was recovering from the Great Depression, and he had to follow the work wherever it took him.

Grandpa knew that he would not be able to give his children the care they needed, so he transferred custody of my dad and his sister to a couple in his family who could not have children of their own. They ended up raising Dad and his sister in Rexburg, Idaho.

Dad was tough as nails and often looking for a fight. When the Korean War broke out, he dropped out of high school to join the navy. Dad was eventually accepted into the Underwater Demolition Team (UDT) program. The UDT frogmen were the predecessors to today's Navy Seals. As a frogman, Dad put his scuba training to use in active-duty warfare operations.

Dad continued his fighting ways in the navy in both sanctioned and unsanctioned bouts. In the military, unsanctioned bouts would often land participants in the brig. I'd be surprised if Dad didn't spend some time there himself for fighting. He did mention that he had done some time on KP duty.

Regardless of whatever trouble Dad might have gotten himself into, he was honorably discharged from the navy after serving four years. Upon his return to civilian life, he enrolled in college at Idaho State University (ISU) in Pocatello, Idaho, where he earned a bachelor's degree in physics.

Mom was born in 1935 in Blackfoot, Idaho, and raised in a blue-collar family in Pocatello. Her dad, my Grandpa Davis, worked as a technician at J.R. Simplot, a local food processing plant. Grandma Davis worked at a local Safeway bakery.

After high school, Mom got a job as a secretary in the math department at ISU. That's where she met Dad. Mom was more of a lover than a fighter. Initially, they were a pretty good match.

Dad and Mom married after a short engagement, and they immediately started a family. They got right to it, having four children in the first five years of their marriage.

The first three children were boys (I was the middle one). After having three boys via three different methods of birth control, my parents were hoping to find something that worked. They didn't really want any more children, but if they were to have any, they would have preferred a girl. So they tried a different method of birth control, and it worked . . . sort of.

Dad and Mom on their wedding day, 1956

My sister was conceived via a fourth method of birth control. Dad and Mom must have eventually found a birth control method that really worked, because they had no more children after my sister.

Mom loved telling that story, but it was actually more than I wanted to know. I didn't want to hear any details of my conception. I didn't want to know any details of my siblings' conceptions, either. I preferred to think of us all being dropped off by a stork.

While my parents both worked to support our family, Dad continued to work on his education. And he continued his fighting ways. Dad boxed as part of a collegiate sports program during his undergraduate years at ISU. I suspect he had his share of unsanctioned fights there, as well.

Besides learning combat, survival, and scuba skills in the navy, Dad learned to party. Perhaps he already knew how to party, but the navy and the friends he made there gave him ample opportunity to sharpen those skills. And drinking would often put Dad in a fighting mood. His drinking and fighting went hand in hand.

Dad went on to earn a master's degree in nuclear physics at Vanderbilt University in Nashville. After graduate school, he went to work in the nuclear industry. In his first job at the Big Rock power plant near Charlevoix, Michigan, Dad used his expertise in scuba diving to train technicians in servicing underwater nuclear reactors.

Later in his career, Dad was considered an expert in the field of radiation health physics. During most of my childhood years, he worked as a health physicist at the National Reactor Testing Station (the Site), about fifty miles west of Idaho Falls.

As an adult, Dad had a few hobbies, including softball, handball, fishing, hunting, and later, skydiving. I wasn't too excited about the skydiving. At that time, parachutes were not as controllable as they are today, and I suspect it was more dangerous. One of Dad's skydiving buddies was missing a few fingers from an earlier mishap. I did get to see a few of Dad's jumps, but I was always a little wary, concerned that each jump could be his last.

For most of his adult life, Dad was a hard drinker. His social activities, including his hobbies, usually involved his drinking buddies. When Dad was sober, he was a kind, loving husband and father, but when he was drunk, he could be mean and volatile.

Dad had a critical nature. I appreciated the constructive criticism he offered when he was sober. It challenged me and made me a better student and a better athlete. But when he was drunk, the criticism was not well-received, not by me, and I suspect not by anyone else.

Mom often worked as a secretary when she was not at home raising us kids. Over the course of her secretarial career, Mom worked in a university math department, a hospital pathology department, and the local sheriff's office. Through those experiences, she saw much of the dark side of life, yet somehow she was always able to see the good in people.

Mom also gave of her time. She served a few years on the PTA board for our local grade school. She also served as Cub Scout den leader for my brothers and me, and a Girl Scout Brownie leader for my sister.

Mom hosted more than her share of birthday parties for us kids, inviting a houseful of neighbor kids to each event. She made our home a neighborhood safe zone. It was warm and welcoming to all.

In contrast to Dad, Mom was always loving and kind. Early in their marriage, Mom encouraged Dad to reconcile with his dad.

When Grandpa's out–of–state work with the railroad was complete, he moved back home and got remarried. After getting settled, Grandpa sought the return of his children from the couple to whom he had transferred custody before beginning his travels. By that time, the couple had become quite fond of Grandpa's children and had taken them in as their own. They were not about to give the children up. In fact, they turned my dad and his sister against Grandpa and his new bride (the woman I would come to know as Grandma Murri).

Mom saw the goodness in Grandpa and Grandma, and helped Dad to see that, too. By the time us kids came around, Dad's relationship with his dad had been restored. As a result I was able to enjoy several years of fishing and hunting with Grandpa. Mom had the ability to see the best in people, and she had a way of bringing them together.

Brett is the oldest of us kids. He and I are Irish twins; in fact, we are just short of eleven months apart. Though we're so close in age, we are miles apart in our personalities and interests.

Brett has more of Mom's personality traits: kind, patient, obedient, and sedentary. I have more of my dad's personality traits: critical, impatient, rebellious, and energetic. Where Brett was drawn to television, movies, books, and band, I was drawn to games, athletics, fishing, and hunting. If I were a little hairier, I'd probably be the Esau to Brett's Jacob. (Look it up in your Bible.)

For the first few years of my life, Brett had the upper hand in our relationship. He led; I followed. When we played cowboys, Brett was always Roy Rogers, and he convinced me to be Dale Evans. I was fine with that because, for all I knew, Dale was just Roy's sidekick, nothing more, nothing less. Later in life, when I learned that Dale Evans was a cow*girl*, I was annoyed that I had been duped into playing the role of a woman.

I doubt that Brett meant any harm in that, but I decided then and there that I would not play the fool again. Putting those early years aside, Brett and I continually vied for the position of top dog, with neither of us yielding to the other.

Throughout our childhood years, Brett was as passive as I was active. He would occasionally play a board game with the rest of us, but he rarely joined us in any of our outdoor activities.

Brett spent a lot of time in front of the television. That seemed like a waste of time to me, but I know that he learned a lot from that. We would occasionally join Brett in watching some of his favorites.

He enjoyed explaining to us what was going on and offered up some relevant background information.

Brett had a few friends in grade school, but they also tended to be more sedentary and liked to watch television with him. I never had much to do with his friends, and he never had much to do with mine. I think Brett would have liked me to join him in his favorite activities as much as I would have liked him to join me in mine. We just couldn't do it; we were too different.

Brett rarely got in trouble. The one time I remember Dad really getting upset with him was one night at the dinner table. Brett was leaning over his plate, his face inches away from the food, shoveling mashed potatoes and gravy into his mouth.

Dad had previously scolded Brett for eating like that and decided to teach him a lesson he wouldn't forget. As Brett went down for another bite, Dad smashed his face into his plate. Brett popped right up, his face plastered with mashed potatoes and gravy. He just sat there for a few moments, stunned, blinking to keep the food out of his eyes.

I started laughing so hard I almost fell off my chair. It wasn't so much the spectacle of Brett's face covered with mashed potatoes and gravy, though that was a funny sight; it was more the recognition that he had actually gotten into trouble. My glee came to an abrupt end when Dad gave me a whoopin' for laughing. Still, I think I'd rather get a whoopin' for laughing than have my face smashed into a plate of mashed potatoes and gravy.

I was kid number two. There's an old Avis car rental company tagline that was popular when I was a kid, "When you're only number two, you try harder." That was certainly true for me. I tried so hard that I got into an awful lot of trouble. I'm certain that I brought most of that on myself, whether it was from disobeying Mom, picking on my sister, or just doing something stupid.

I remember getting into trouble for burning a hole in the garden hose shortly after we moved to the new place. Dad gave me a whoopin' for that, but I really didn't think I had anything to do with it. Never mind the fact that I was the only one in the house with a magnifying glass.

I had recently discovered that my magnifying glass could be used to focus enough of the sun's energy to burn ants. I acknowledge it's possible that an ant could have been crawling along the hose when it caught my attention. And it's certainly within the realm of possibilities that, in that unique situation, with all of my focus putting all of the sun's focus on the ant, the hose may have been burned as part of the collateral damage.

Is it possible that I burned the hose? Yes. Did I think it likely that I burned the hose? No. Presented with these facts today, I'd have to plead the fifth.

At one point, I was tired of being blamed for everything (deservedly, or not), so I decided to run away from home. I wanted to go somewhere safe, yet not far from my supply line for food, water, and comfort. I wanted to be able to hear when my family came searching for me, sobbing and calling out my name.

The scoreboard box behind our house seemed like the perfect spot. So early one morning, I made my way out there, shinnied up the fence, and climbed in, completely undetected. There I sat, and waited, and waited, and waited.

Nobody came looking for me. I was thinking, *How could they not be missing me?*

By the end of the day, I was starving and probably needing a little love. I would have liked to hold my ground until someone came begging me to come home. I wanted to make my point that I was so often mistreated. But I caved.

Later in life, in my college psychology class, I would learn about Maslow's hierarchy of needs. My physiological need for food was greater than my need for love and belonging. So, it wasn't my fault that I caved. I really had no choice.

In silent surrender, I climbed down from my secret little hideaway in the scoreboard box and went home for dinner. When I walked through the door, nobody came running to greet me or hug me or ask me where I had been all day. Nobody even seemed to know or care that I had been gone.

When Mom saw me, the only thing she had to say was, "Go wash your hands and sit down for dinner."

"Okay, Mom," I replied. I was famished and happy to oblige her.

That marked both the beginning and the end of my runaway days.

Brice came into the picture a few years after me. He has a good blend of Mom's and Dad's personality traits. He's fairly quiet, patient, and easygoing, but he is also very energetic and driven.

Initially, Brice just sort of bumped along and got lots of attention from adults because he was so cute. For the most part, he just stayed out of my way. With two years between us, we didn't have a whole lot to do with each other.

Shortly after the move, that all changed. Brice morphed in my eyes from an almost non-existent little brother to an open–for–adventure, fun–loving tagalong.

Brice and I soon became cohorts in crime. When Mom yelled at us for whatever mischief we were up to, I would protest and usually end up in trouble. Brice, on the other hand, would agree to do or not do whatever it was she was yelling about.

While I was receiving the brunt of Mom's wrath, Brice would just continue with whatever it was he was doing or not doing, as if Mom hadn't said a thing. Ultimately, I would yield to Mom's authority.

Mom would walk away happy and content, having laid down the law and getting us straightened out. I'd walk away from the exchange all bruised and battered, figuratively speaking, having lost another battle to the maker of rules.

Brice managed to avoid the fray; he seemed to enjoy just being a spectator in the battle. As I reflect back on that now, I realize that Brice was allowing me to run interference for him. As long as I was there to draw Mom's fire, he could do whatever he wanted.

As an older brother, I could easily take Brice down when we were kids (as in a wrestling take down), but I could never get him to surrender. He was a *stubborn* little kid. I only recall us having one significant dispute, and that was when he sic'd his dog on me.

I had just come home from school and leaned over to pet the dog. Though it was a family pet, we all knew it was really Brice's dog. That dog had more loyalty to Brice than to the rest of us combined. I don't know what possessed Brice, and I doubt that he knows himself, but as I was petting the dog, Brice commanded, "Sic 'em." The stinking dog obeyed and bit me on the lip.

I was instantly enraged. I was mad at the dog and smacked it right away. But the dog was just obeying a command. So then I punched Brice in the face, hard. I was in pretty good shape then, and I probably didn't know my own strength. Brice ended up with a very swollen, very black eye.

When Mom got home and saw Brice's swollen eye, she gave me a good talkin' to, but it wasn't really necessary. After calming down and realizing what I had done, I felt horrible enough as it was. I didn't intend to seriously hurt my little buddy. I resolved to better control my emotional and physical response in the future.

At one point in our younger years, Mom mentioned to Brice and me, out of the blue, that Grandpa Davis had come from Viking heritage. Whether or not that's true is still a matter of dispute. DNA ancestry testing has only confirmed Viking heritage as a possibility, with genetic links to Great Britain, Finland, and Scandinavia. But that casual statement had far–reaching ramifications.

Brice and I took that statement as gospel truth. Believing that we had Viking blood helped us through a lot of difficult and challenging times, like when our parents eventually split up. Vikings were tough, so we were tough. Vikings didn't get hurt, so we didn't get hurt—not that we would admit it. Vikings didn't cry, so we didn't cry—not where anyone would see it. Having Viking blood is still an inside joke in our family.

Brenda was the youngest child and only girl. As such, she was the cute little princess who could do no wrong. The rules that Mom laid down for us boys didn't always apply to Brenda.

On one occasion, when Brenda was old enough to know better, she knocked a blind down from the window and told Mom that a fly did it. Brenda never got in trouble for it, not even for lying (the cardinal sin). Maybe I'm not being fair. I suppose it's possible that it really *was* the fly's fault.

Whether knowingly or not, Mom babied her little princess. Brenda never had to do anything she didn't want to do.

Mom put all of us kids in swim lessons at an early age. Having a Navy Seal for a dad, none of us really had much choice. We were all going to learn to swim. All of us, that is, except for Brenda.

We all took lessons for several summers, and us boys learned to swim pretty well. Brenda splashed around for a few lessons, but she didn't like it, so Mom pulled her out. Brenda never did learn to swim.

I went through my childhood being mostly annoyed with Brenda, though it was through no fault of her own. I believe my annoyance can be most directly attributed to the special treatment she got from Mom. Whether it was for that reason, or something else, I was always picking on Brenda. To me, it was all in fun. It wasn't meant to be hurtful, but it probably was hurtful and not much fun for her.

At times, Brice would also get annoyed with Brenda. On one occasion, he was so annoyed that he sprayed insecticide in her mouth. Though I could relate to his frustration, that was a bridge too far. I was sincerely concerned for Brenda's well-being.

Mom called the hospital, and they gave her some instruction on what to look for and how to counteract the poison. Brenda survived that ordeal with no lasting effects other than a strong distaste for insecticide. Brice got the worst of it with a well–deserved whoopin'.

The one time I recall Brenda doing something that I thought would get her in trouble, I was almost giddy. Unfortunately, it didn't quite work out the way I expected.

Brenda and I were going door to door in the neighborhood selling apples from our tree. We didn't get too far before we were being buzzed by a swarm of yellow jackets. Apparently, the yellow jackets were more interested in our apples than our neighbors had been—our sales had been lackluster, at best.

Brenda could only put up with the swarming wasps for so long before she let loose with some words that she must have heard from Dad's mouth.

With the sound of exasperation, Brenda yelled out, "Those sons–a–bitchin' bees!"

In our house, cussing by anyone under the age of thirty was a soap–in–the–mouth offense. I threatened to expose this infraction to Mom unless Brenda did everything I asked. I don't think I was too overly demanding. How hard is it to fan someone and feed them grapes?

After a couple of days, Brenda broke down and told Mom what happened. That ended with a whoopin' for me, and once again, no consequences for Brenda. Mom felt that Brenda had already paid for her crime, having endured two days of extortion at my hand. In that situation, Mom was probably right.

Though I was always in trouble for picking on Brenda, I also served as her protector. When the situation required, I took that role quite seriously. To my mind, it was okay for *me* to pick on Brenda, but it was not okay for anyone outside the family.

In grade school, some kid made the mistake of intentionally popping Brenda's helium balloon at a Halloween carnival. That kid ended up with a black eye.

I watched out for my sister in other ways, too, like walking her to and from her dance lessons. Sitting through those lessons was boring as all get out, but I really didn't mind serving as her bodyguard and escort.

My closest friends had little sisters who were about the same age as Brenda. When my friends came over, they would often bring their sisters along. That way, the girls could play together, have their own fun, and stay out of our hair.

All things considered, I liked having a little sister. I just didn't appreciate the special treatment she got from Mom, and I didn't want her interfering with me and my friends.

Brenda, me, Brice, and Brett, circa 1965
(about the time of our move)

CHAPTER 4

BURNT COOKIES

Most of us are familiar with the expression, "Home is where the heart is." Though there's not much supporting documentation, this idiom is attributed to Pliny the Elder (AD 23–79). Whether first spoken by Pliny the Elder, Pliny the Younger, or someone not named Pliny, the expression is from time immemorial. Note that the expression specifically refers to the home, not to the cave, not to the castle, not to the house.

We might appreciate various aspects of the places where we've lived, and we may feel somewhat nostalgic to go back and visit, but our hearts are not there. Our hearts are with our homes, the families and others with whom we have shared our lives in those places. I'd like to tell you about my house—my home.

We quickly adjusted to life in the new house. Initially, Brett and I shared one bedroom, while Brice and Brenda shared another.

We learned to make do with the one bathroom. Dad had his undisturbed time first thing in the morning, as he had to get up early to go to work. Before any of us kids got up, he'd be out the door and off to the

Site bus stop, from which contracted buses would transport employees to the National Reactor Test Station.

Mom was up early, too, but she gave us boys next dibs on the bathroom as soon as we were up. We were able to share nicely without getting in each other's way. We could triple team the shower, if necessary, and double team the toilet in emergency situations of the number one order. We allowed privacy for a number two situation, but we were all quick about it.

Mom would get her time in the bathroom after we were all out the door for school. If anyone got the short end of the stick, it was Brenda. Later in life, Brenda would have plenty of bathroom time to herself when all of us boys left home for college and careers.

In general, with only one bathroom, it was get in and get out. There was no time for camping out, and never any reading material around like you might see in some families' bathrooms. If by chance any reading material would have shown up, us kids would have assumed it was only for backup in case the TP ran out.

Several years into living in the new house, Dad was making decent money, so we no longer needed renters to help out with the mortgage. Dad and Mom were able to make good on their promise for us to expand into the rental unit.

As the oldest kid, Brett got the unit to himself. The only stipulation was that he share "his" bathroom with anyone and everyone in need. Brice moved into the bedroom with me, further cementing our already close relationship, while Brenda got the other bedroom all to herself (not surprising). Mom painted the walls of Brenda's bedroom pink, and the two of them turned it into a beauty salon, more or less. That essentially made it a "no go" zone for me and my friends.

Dad derived a lot of pleasure from the two–way access linen cabinet between the hallway and bathroom. He exploited that feature to surprise our unsuspecting male guests. It didn't matter whether the guests were family, friend, or foe; all were fair game.

If we were expecting guests who had not been to the new house before, Dad would prop open the linen cabinet doors on the bathroom side before anyone arrived. When the guests showed up, he would greet them with a warm welcome, sit them down in the entertainment room, and ply them with alcohol. For teetotalers, just about any non-alcoholic beverage would do.

Dad would keep the guests entertained until one of them would eventually have to get up to answer nature's call. The guest would excuse himself and head off to the bathroom to do his business. As soon as the bathroom door closed, Dad would hasten to the hallway. There, he would listen for just the right moment, then swing open the hall side cabinet doors to catch the unsuspecting party midstream. If the gentleman's back was to the linen cabinet (which was most often the case), Dad would startle him with a loud, abrupt greeting.

Dad had that little caper down to an art. Mom was not at all amused with it. I suspect that's because she had to clean the bathroom toilet and floor more frequently as a result.

Dad was very much at home in the entertainment room. That's where he could go to find peace and quiet at the end of a long workday. He would come home, fix himself a martini, put his feet up, and browse through the local newspaper. That was his way of unwinding. It was clear to us kids that Dad was not to be disturbed during that time. Whatever disturbance we had queued up would have to wait until after dinner.

High fidelity (hi-fi) stereo systems were hitting the market about that time, and Dad had to have one. A little background music, of nothing but the highest quality, would add a nice ambiance to his little corner of heaven, which was essentially a man cave.

After shopping around, Dad decided that he would build his own hi-fi stereo system. I don't know whether that was due to the high cost of an off–the–shelf system, or he just wanted the challenge of building his own. Either way, he was determined to build one himself.

Dad ordered a hi-fi stereo system kit from the Heath Company. The Heathkit came complete with parts and detailed assembly instructions for building an amplifier, a pair of speakers, and a turntable (a.k.a. phonograph).

Dad was not what you would call a handy man. Building a stereo system would be quite an undertaking for him. He didn't have much in the way of tools, so he had to buy a few specific items to get started, including a soldering iron, a pair of needle–nosed pliers, and an assortment of small screwdrivers.

Dad spent nearly every waking hour working on that project, from the time the kit arrived until it was complete several months later. When the last screw was installed and tightened, it was time for the smoke test (i.e., powering it up).

Dad closed his eyes and flipped the switch. There was no smoke or smell of burning electronics. There were no blown fuses. Those were good signs. Then came the ultimate test.

We held our breath in silence as Dad gently placed his favorite Sons of the Pioneers record on the turntable, hit play, and . . . *voilà*. The silence was broken with the melancholy ballad of "Tumbling Tumbleweeds" reverberating around the room.

It worked! Dad's homebuilt stereo system actually worked! We were all astounded. Dad had outdone himself. He cranked up the volume and let the tumbleweeds roll, smiling like a little kid. That homebuilt hi-fi stereo system was literally music to his ears. He loved showing it off to family and friends.

Despite all the time and effort Dad spent working on his pride and joy (the hi-fi stereo system), it had one minor defect. The turntable's stylus needed some additional weight, the weight of a single copper penny, to keep it from occasionally skipping across the grooves of his vinyl records. It may have been a minor defect, but to Dad, it was a major irritation. Sure, the penny worked. It just didn't look professional.

Dad tried everything he could to fix the defect some other way (e.g., adjusting the height of the tonearm, changing out the stylus, etc.). Nothing else worked. In the end, he admitted defeat and resigned himself to permanently gluing a penny to the top of the stylus. The penny was a constant reminder of that single minor flaw, but it added a little character to Dad's high fidelity conversation piece.

Mom was drawn in by the lilac bushes that adorned the front side of the new house. Flowers from the lilac bushes produced Mom's favorite fragrance in the whole wide world. The lilacs flowered every spring, with the heaviest blooms usually occurring in May.

Mom kept a continual bouquet of fresh lilac flowers in the house for as long as they were in bloom. She wanted to take in as much of that sweet floral aroma as humanly possible. If she could have captured it and bottled it up to enjoy throughout the year, she would have. Mom didn't get too upset if we damaged or destroyed other flowers and shrubs around the place, but if we messed with her lilacs, there'd be hell to pay.

Mom also loved her new kitchen. It was bigger than what she was used to, and she had it stocked with all of the appliances, small and large, that you would ever need for modern living.

Why Mom loved that kitchen so much is hard to say. I don't believe it was from a love for cooking. If you love doing something, you tend to do it well. Mom did not do cooking well. She had a lot of skills, but cooking was not one of them. I suspect her love for the kitchen had more to do with the telephone or the dining room window.

The telephone, which hung on the kitchen wall near the oven, was Mom's lifeline to the outside world. With four young kids born in a five–year span, Mom needed that lifeline. She needed adult conversation, and most any adult would do.

For the first several years in that house, the telephone handset had a cord that might have stretched five feet, at best. The short cord meant that you would essentially be confined to a small section of the kitchen while talking on the phone.

Mom wore out the linoleum floor in that small section of the kitchen just below where the telephone was hung. That was her happy place. Mom later replaced the short cord with one that would stretch over twenty feet. That greatly expanded her reach and provided her with more options for multitasking while talking on the phone.

The dining room window offered Mom another lifeline to the outside world. She could sit at the dining room table with a warm drink in hand (or a stiff drink in hand, depending on her state of mind), look out the window, and daydream of what life might be like without us kids around. I know Mom loved us, and she loved being a mom, but I also know that we represented a ball and chain around her ankle.

Whether it was the phone, the dining room window, or something else that drew Mom to the kitchen, I don't know for certain. What I do know for certain is that, in the new kitchen, Mom had room for more pots, pans, dishes, and trays to burn things in.

In Mom's kitchen, we usually started our day with a cold breakfast (e.g., cereal, toast, Hostess donuts). On a rare occasion, Mom would cook us up some bacon, eggs, and toast. She had every intention of making it to order, but regardless of how it was ordered, it all came out the same: eggs, over hard; bacon, extra crispy; toast, dark brown.

On cold, wintery days, Mom would prepare one of two hot drinks for us kids, either hot cocoa, or hot Jell-O water. Hot cocoa may not be all that nutritious, but it's a tasty, perfectly normal hot beverage. There's no rational reason why you couldn't have hot cocoa each and every cold, wintery day.

For some *irrational* reason, we didn't have hot cocoa each and every cold, wintery day. Mom felt compelled to mix things up a bit. She included hot Jell-O water in the rotation of hot drinks that she would prepare for us.

Hot Jell-O water is not normal; it can't be that nutritious, and it just tastes awful. Choose any flavor you want, stir in some boiling water, serve it hot, and it's still awful. Where did Mom come up with that idea? Was it field tested? Did Mikey like it? I don't think so.

Drinking hot Jell-O water went against every ounce of natural instinct I had. Its only redeeming value was to make the pre-colonoscopy cleanse that I would have to drink later in life a little easier to swallow.

Lunch would usually consist of PBJs or cheese sandwiches. On cold days, Mom might throw in some hot Campbell's soup for good measure. I think the hot soup helped to keep the Jell-O water from prematurely coagulating in our stomachs.

When we got to junior high, Mom would occasionally give us money to buy our lunch. We could buy hot lunch at the nearby high school cafeteria for a very reasonable price. There were also a few fast-food joints close to school if we wanted to splurge. Buying our lunch was a treat compared to what we were used to, and it helped us learn to budget.

Mom made sure we ate dinner together most every night. She intended that as an opportunity to hear how everyone's day went. Talk would usually start on a high note, but it often devolved into a gripe session over some part of the meal. With six picky eaters and one bad cook, there was bound to be someone complaining about something. Even Mom got into the act, recognizing that her cooking left a lot to be desired.

Mom did have a few specialties in her repertoire that she would prepare from time to time. Those were good, but they were also few and far between. Most of our dinners were from cans (e.g., vegetables, chow mein), mixes (e.g., Hamburger Helper, Tuna Helper), or the freezer (e.g., TV dinners, meat pies).

On a very rare occasion, Mom or Dad would bring home some takeout food. We lived for takeout. If it wasn't for the high school cafeteria and restaurants with takeout, I don't think my tastebuds would have ever matured.

Dad didn't spend much time in the kitchen. That was Mom's domain. However, he had a charcoal grill with an electric rotisserie feature, and he knew how to use it. He could grill up most any meat and cook it just right.

Mom tried her hand with chicken on the grill once, but when it was done, it looked like it had come out of a crematorium. After that, Mom's cooking was strictly confined to the kitchen, where the odds of us getting an edible meal were slightly higher.

Dad's other specialty in food preparation was jerky. He would marinate strips of venison in a large, galvanized steel tub in the laundry room for a few days, and then hang it to dry on Mom's clothesline.

The jerky was good; not great, but good. The flavor was decent, which accounted for the "good" rating. But it was tough as nails. That kept it from getting a "great" rating. Dad's venison jerky was sort of like a savory stick of gum. You could chew on a single piece all day long.

On one occasion, after all of us kids had been passing around one flu bug after another, Mom decided to cook up a brew that would supposedly cure us of all that ailed us. Mom was hoping this special brew would 1) make us all feel better, and 2) help us to not miss any more school. I'm pretty sure she had no recipe for her special brew; she just made it up.

The brew was a pot full of fruits, vegetables, spices, and other various and sundry items that Mom pulled out of the kitchen cabinets. She literally boiled and stirred it all day long. As it boiled, a noxious cloud wafted through the air, steaming up the kitchen windows, and permeating the house with a most disagreeable odor.

The brew smelled horrible, and it tasted worse. It was even worse than hot Jell-O water, if you can imagine that. We all had to drink a cup of it. I can't speak for the others, but I honestly did my best and choked it down, stifling my natural gag reflex with each sip. Mom ended up dumping most of it out at the end of the day.

I don't believe Mom's special brew made us any healthier, but it did accomplish its two purposes, though not as Mom had intended: we all immediately felt better, knowing that the worst was over. We would no longer have to smell or taste that nasty brew. And we didn't miss any more school for the remainder of that cold and flu season. We went to school, whether we were sick or not. It was better to go to school feeling like crap than to run the risk of having Mom cook up another batch of that stuff.

Mom learned to be resourceful. She had to. Her shopping days were before the invention of credit cards, so she couldn't just charge her groceries and figure out how to pay for them later.

We didn't qualify for food stamps, either. Like other homemakers in her time, Mom had to pay for whatever groceries she bought with whatever funds she had on hand, in cash or in her checking account.

Coupons really came into prominence in the late fifties, and Mom was a coupon–clipping queen. She could stretch her dollars with those coupons like no other.

I pity the shoppers who ended up in line behind Mom on her major grocery shopping days. After ringing up every item in her over-filled cart, the checkers would have to review and enter each coupon, manually. More often than not, the checker would have to call for a price check or a manager's assistance with a coupon or some item that was supposed to be on sale and wasn't ringing up as such.

Mom was also able to stretch her grocery dollars by purchasing items either on sale or in bulk. She picked up a used chest freezer for a reasonable price and used that to store perishable bulk foods.

Mom was a regular patron at the local Hostess day–old store. The chest freezer was always filled with various Hostess pastries. Those frozen pastries were fair game for after–school snacks.

I'm sure Mom had some healthy options on hand, like apples and oranges, but if we wanted something that we thought tasted good, the Hostess pastries were our go to. Of course we never thought to thaw anything out ahead of time. And since microwave ovens had not been invented yet, we had no choice but to eat the pastries in their frozen state. I usually opted for a frozen Hostess fruit pie. I could gnaw on one of those for hours.

Mom did a lot of her shopping at Russ's Market. She would make regular trips there to stock up, but from time to time she'd send us kids to pick up a few last–minute items.

On one occasion, Mom was going to be entertaining some guests for dinner, but she was afraid she'd run out of napkins. She sent me to the store to get some, and I took Brenda along.

Brenda and I had no idea where in the store to look for napkins. We had walked up and down several aisles and were beginning to get discouraged. The napkins were not jumping out at us.

We eventually came across some packages labeled feminine napkins. I knew that the word *feminine* implied that it was for girls.

It didn't bother me that we didn't see any masculine napkins, knowing that the word *masculine* implied it was for guys, because I figured most guys don't care about napkins. My brothers and I would usually just wipe our hands on our jeans.

It made sense to me that the label would indicate that the package contained napkins for girls. Brenda agreed with me on that logic.

We bought the smallest pack of feminine napkins they had because they were fairly expensive, and we knew Mom didn't need a lot. Then we set off for home with our heads held high, having accomplished the mission, and having spent Mom's money wisely.

When we arrived back home and Mom saw what we bought, she nearly broke down in hysterics. She wouldn't explain to us why she was laughing, nor would she tell us why she couldn't place those particular napkins around the table for our dinner guests. For some reason, Mom never sent me to the store to purchase napkins again.

Mom did do some baking, a skill she came close to, but didn't quite arrive at learning from her mom (Grandma Davis). Mom understood the general concepts of baking; she just didn't execute well. Where grandma's baked goods were cooked to perfection (to a nice, golden brown), Mom had a talent for routinely overcooking hers (to somewhere between ebony and onyx).

I shouldn't complain; we always had food on our table and/or in the freezer. We just needed to adjust our attitudes and tastebuds ever so slightly to appreciate Mom's style of cooking. Over time, my siblings and I all developed a taste for dry cake, burnt cookies, and frozen pies. It wasn't until later in my adult life that I would come to truly appreciate a freshly baked, warm apple pie, with a flaky, golden brown crust.

CHAPTER 5

SUNDAY DRIVES

"The family that plays together, stays together." So goes the anonymous quote. And it's true; there *is* value in families just spending time together, especially when it involves something everyone enjoys. But what really bonds families together is shared crises. Gary Smalley said that if you want to build closer family relationships, go camping.[4] The idea is that if you go camping enough—and it doesn't usually take many outings—at some point you will encounter adversity.

Working through adversity, or shared crises, will draw a family closer together. I dedicate this chapter to Mom and Dad for helping us work our way through a lot of shared crises, some of which they got us into in the first place!

Our family time included an occasional Sunday drive. When the weather was nice, and there were no football games to watch on television, Dad would pile us all into his 1950s vintage Nissan Patrol, and we'd head for the hills. The Nissan Patrol was a basic, pine–green four–wheel–drive Jeep-type vehicle with transverse–mounted bench seats in the back. All four of us kids would sit in the back, facing each other, with a dog or two thrown in for good measure.

Our Sunday drives nearly always involved some amount of rough terrain and winding mountain roads. I suppose that goes without saying, since after all, it *was* an all-terrain vehicle.

In those days, Mom sported a beehive hairdo that was held together and in place with about a quart of hairspray. Despite all of the lacquer, Mom believed that any amount of wind blowing across her head could lead to the beehive's undoing. Therefore, opening a window to allow for some fresh air was out of the question. Of course, we couldn't turn on air conditioning because the Nissan Patrol didn't have any.

Under those conditions alone (stale air, hair spray, sweaty bodies, and dog breath), it was smelly and suffocating. Blend in a continuous exhaust of cigarette smoke (besides being a heavy drinker, Dad was a chain smoker), and you start to get the picture of what our Sunday drives were like. To add insult to injury, Dad would have country music blaring on the radio.

I grew to detest those Sunday drives. To this day, it pains me to hear the words *Sunday* and *drive* in the same sentence. I will only drive (or be driven) if I have a reason to get from point A to point B, and I will always take the shortest route possible.

On warm days, I prefer to have the windows rolled down; A/C is acceptable, but fresh air is preferred. I still get nauseous when I detect the least amount of cigarette smoke in the air. I do everything I can to avoid rental cars and hotel rooms that have been used by smokers.

For the longest time, I had a strong disdain for country music. As an adult, I eventually gained an appreciation for it. I can now listen to and enjoy country music without subconsciously getting carsick.

Birthdays, holidays, and other special occasions for our family were probably not a lot different from most everyone else's. We'd usually get together with a bunch of relatives, and there would be lots of good food. Whether it was Mom's side of the family or Dad's, it usually meant us driving an hour each way to one of their homes.

I hated riding in the car for any length of time, but at least there was a point to it. We weren't driving just for the sake of driving. And not long after we arrived, I would be just fine. Whatever nausea I had would quickly dissipate as I took in the various aromas emanating from the kitchen.

We often made the trip from Idaho Falls to Pocatello (about an hour's drive) to spend time with my Mom's parents, Grandma and Grandpa Davis. Grandma had a special drawer where she kept a supply of day–old donuts on hand for us kids. In reality, I believe those donuts were often as much as a week old, but to us kids, a donut was a donut.

We would occasionally get to visit grandma at the bakery, where we'd receive a behind–the–scenes tour. At the end of the tour, we'd be rewarded with fresh, warm donuts, right off the cooling rack.

Grandma and Grandpa Davis were the first of anyone we knew to own a color television. It was one of those big console television sets that make great boat anchors today, if you can find one. Anyway, when the Apollo 11 astronauts were preparing to walk on the moon, we drove the hour to their place just to watch the broadcast in color. That trip was worth the drive. The whole experience was surreal. As we were watching, I realized how fortunate I was to live in what we have come to know as the space age.

Grandma and Grandpa Davis loved watching *The Lawrence Welk Show*. They dreamed of one day seeing one of their grandkids perform on it. Mom tried to oblige them by putting all of us boys in accordion lessons. I suppose since Brenda was taking dance lessons, she was exempt.

Each week, Brett, Brice, and I would drag our rented accordions out of the closet, go to our lesson where we'd be chastised for not practicing, suffer through whatever the instructor was trying to teach us, and return home to stuff the accordions back into the closet. And there the accordions would sit, undisturbed, gathering dust until the next week's lesson.

That scenario was repeated, week after week for several months. Mom hated to give up on the whole Lawrence Welk thing, but she eventually recognized that it was a complete waste of her time and money. The day Mom took those accordions back to the rental shop was one of the happiest days of my young life. In hindsight, my time would have been better spent in dance lessons with Brenda.

Grandma and Grandpa Murri had a boat, and they loved to fish. We were invited to join them on many an occasion. They'd take our family to their favorite fishing spot on Henry's Lake, where us kids would catch fish until our hands were swollen and we could no longer hold a pole or spin a reel. Dad was happy, angry, and frustrated all at the same time because he could barely keep up putting bait on our hooks, casting our lines, taking fish off our hooks, and untangling our lines. He had no opportunity to fish himself, and he loved to fish.

After we had our fill of fishing, we would transition to water sports. Us boys would take to waterskiing, while Mom and Brenda would sit on the dock and look pretty.

Most every outing, Dad would show off his body skimming maneuver, a stunt that he had learned in the navy. He'd sit on the side edge of the boat with no one else on board but the driver. When the boat hit top speed (approaching 30 mph), Dad would tuck into a fetal position and roll off the side, facing upward with his back to the water. In that position, he would bounce and skim along the surface of the water quite a ways until gradually coming to a stop. At that point, he would have to swim or tread water until the boat could get back to pick him up.

On at least one occasion, Dad's swim trunks were torn off on initial impact with the water. Mom would bring along an extra pair of Dad's swim trunks to keep him modest in those situations.

As we got a little older, Dad would take Brett and me deer hunting. We completed an NRA hunter education course and began hunting at the earliest opportunity. With fall birthdays, we were each barely twelve years old when we went on our first hunts.

On my first hunt, Dad had me walk down a ravine while he hunted the ridge above. I now realize that he essentially had me dogging for him: Dad was the hunter; I was the dog. We started walking within sight of each other, about 100 yards apart. As we hiked, the timber got thicker, and it was getting harder for me to keep Dad in view. After I had lost sight of him for what seemed like an eternity, but in all likelihood was only ten or fifteen minutes, I began to panic. I thought I was lost. So, as I learned in my hunter education class, I fired off three rounds in rapid succession to indicate that I was lost.

The normal response for someone hearing three shots fired in rapid succession would be to fire off two rounds in rapid succession to acknowledge that they heard and understood. There was no response. Dad knew exactly where I was; I wasn't far. He just assumed I had spooked up a deer and was shooting at it, so he stopped and stood quietly for several minutes.

Something else I learned in hunter education was to stay put when you think you're lost. So I did that, too. Dad soon made his way down to me. He asked what I was shooting at. He wasn't happy when I told him I wasn't shooting at anything. I was shooting because I thought I was lost. He shook his head, put his arm around me, and we headed back up the hill to the ol' Nissan Patrol.

All the way home I was schooled on the techniques of walking through the timber, staying the course, and remaining calm. So ended my first hunt. The deer would live to see another day.

On a subsequent hunting trip that year, with Dad keeping me close by, we stopped at the top of a mesa to scope the valley below. We spotted a small herd of deer, several hundred yards away. We each got into a comfortable shooting position, and on Dad's signal, we opened fire.

Dad had a 30-06 Remington bolt action rifle with scope. Brett had 30-30 Remington bolt action rifle with scope. I had a Winchester 30-30 lever action rifle with iron sights (no scope). I loved that rifle because it was the same as Little Joe Cartwright used in *Bonanza*. My rifle may have looked cool, but with no scope, it put me at a disadvantage. I was no match for the shooting accuracy Dad and Brett had with their rifles.

We were able to fire off a few rounds each before the deer all bolted away. When the shooting stopped, it wasn't clear to me that any of our shots had hit their mark. We walked down to the valley floor as quick as we could go. Our speed of descent was directly proportional to our age, so Dad was the first down, and I was last.

Just before I reached the bottom, I heard another gunshot. By the time I got to Dad, he was in the process of dressing out a deer. When he saw me, he stood up and congratulated me on my fine shooting. He said that he saw the deer go down immediately after one of my shots, so he was certain it was mine.

I was beaming with pride as I gave the deer a quick look over. I bent down to help Dad finish field dressing *my* deer, all the while trying to brush aside any emotional attachment to it. As we were working, Dad casually mentioned that I had hit it in the butt. That meant that a significant amount of meat was ruined.

Nobody wants to make a butt shot. It's sort of like kissing your sister, but a little messier. I wasn't happy about it, but it *was* my first deer. In my mind, it still counted.

Over time, I came to realize it was very unlikely that I had hit that deer. I was the least experienced hunter, and I had the least accurate firearm (sans scope) for that kind of distance. With all of us shooting at the same time, how could Dad have possibly seen the deer go down after one of my shots? I don't believe he did.

So why would Dad have given me the credit for it? Because he knew that it would make me happy to have shot my first deer, regardless of where it was hit, he wouldn't have to take me hunting again that season, and he would still have a valid tag to continue hunting, himself. I think a jury of my peers would have found me innocent of shooting that deer.

Other than a few fishing, hunting, and camping trips, the only real family vacations we took were road trips to Disneyland. We went twice. Mom said the only reason Dad agreed to those trips was so that he could spend some time in Las Vegas on the way. He liked the gambling and the shows. If that's what it took for us to go to Disneyland, great! We were all for it and happy that Dad agreed to take us.

One of the best parts of those vacations was getting to dine out at restaurants along the way. On one of our Disneyland road trips, we stopped at a pancake house for breakfast. It was one of those chain restaurants that has since closed because it had a politically incorrect name.

Brice and Brenda both got a large plate of chocolate pancakes, piled high with chocolate pudding and whipped cream, which neither one could finish. Brett got a plate of waffles, but it wasn't very filling, so he helped to finish off Brice and Brenda's chocolate pancakes. He completely stuffed himself. It was too good to let any go to waste. I stuffed myself, too, but not with chocolate pancakes.

After breakfast, we loaded back up into our Oldsmobile station wagon and continued on down the road, through the hot Sierra Nevada desert. The station wagon didn't have air conditioning. Mom still sported her beehive hairdo, and Dad still chain-smoked. It was hot, stuffy, and smoky.

Brett started to feel a little carsick and complained of feeling nauseous. Mom offered him a Pepsi to help settle his stomach. Whatever ice we had in the cooler had long since melted, so none of the drinks were cold. Brett guzzled down some warm Pepsi. That only made things worse.

A few miles down the road, up came a bubbly mix of partially digested waffles, chocolate pancakes, chocolate pudding, cream that had formerly been whipped, and Pepsi. The smell was putrid. A few of us other kids were starting to get sick.

Before anyone else could spill their cookies—or pancakes, as it were—Dad pulled the car over and had everyone get out. While we were all out walking around and breathing in some fresh air, Mom was taking one for the team, doing what she could to clean it up. Mom and Dad agreed that chocolate pancakes would be banned for all future road trips.

This may sound cliché, but our trips to Disneyland were magical. When we took our first trip, Disneyland was fairly new; it had only been open for ten years or so. As with most first–time visitors, we had never experienced anything like it.

We were able to enjoy most of what the top–rated amusement park had to offer. Many of the rides we took then are still in operation today, including It's a Small World, Pirates of the Caribbean, and the Jungle Cruise. The mechanized animals we saw on the Jungle Cruise seemed so real, especially since us kids had never seen many of those animals in real life, at a park, zoo, or anywhere else.

We all got some kind of hat as a souvenir. Brice's Donald Duck hat was the most memorable. It had a bill that would quack when squeezed, and it was apparently irresistible to passersby. Everyone and their dog had to squeeze it. Brice loved the hat, but he did not love the constant invasion of his personal space.

Those trips to Disneyland were true vacations. We all got along better than ever. Both trips gave us an opportunity to bond more closely together as a family.

Like those few Disneyland vacations, Christmas time always provided an opportunity for family bonding. When it came to Christmas, Mom was very much given to tradition. For her, the Christmas season began the day after Thanksgiving, and lasted until sometime well after New Year's Day. Mom would decorate the house as best she could with what little she had.

Mom made sure we had a *real* Christmas tree each year, brimming with ornaments, lights, and tinsel. One year, she even tried a do–it–yourself Christmas tree frost kit, but that didn't go so well. We ended up having to get our carpet cleaned after the tree was taken down.

Just about every day during the Christmas season, Mom would play Christmas music from the time we got up in the morning until the time we went to bed at night, everything from Julie Andrews to the Singing Nun to Alvin and the Chipmunks.

Every year, Mom would bake sugar cookies using Christmas–themed cutouts, and she would have us frost them. She encouraged us to use lots of frosting to cover the burnt ones, especially when they were used in cookie exchanges with neighbors and friends. We went through a lot of icing.

Gifts were Mom's love language. On both the giving and the receiving end, gifts were her way of expressing love. And nothing beats

Christmas when it comes to giving and receiving gifts. Mom would shower us kids with gifts and fill our stockings to the top with candy and all sorts of knick knacks from the five and dime. For her it was more about the quantity than the quality, but for us as for most kids, quantity was good.

A tradition in our home was that we would each choose one gift to open on Christmas Eve. We'd open the remaining gifts on Christmas morning. I'm guessing that tradition got started because Mom and Dad would usually go out on Christmas Eve, and they could keep us entertained playing with whatever we had opened that evening.

A few years into that tradition, I decided that I didn't want to open anything the night before. I wanted to "save my fun," all of it, for Christmas morning. (I know, I was a weird kid.) Mom couldn't understand that. She would want to open a gift just as soon as she had the chance, and she assumed everyone felt the same.

I was informed that opening a gift on Christmas Eve was not just a tradition, it was a rule. For another year or two, I reluctantly chose a gift, and dutifully opened it the night before Christmas. I followed the rule just like everyone else.

Then came the Christmas Eve when I had an epiphany. As I was surveying the packages from which to choose, I remembered that one of my aunts almost always gave us boys a bundle of underwear. My sister would get a doll or a tea party set or something else that little girls like, but us boys would all get underwear.

That year, with a Grinch–like gleam in my eye, I chose the package that would most certainly be another bundle of tighty whities. I tore off the wrapping as quick as I could, and there they were. Three pair of brand–new Fruit of the Looms in one nicely packaged little bundle. Who would have guessed it?

For the first time ever, I was actually excited to open a package of underwear. The truth is, I hated getting underwear, but I was excited because I had just scored a hat trick:

    1) I satisfied the "open a present on Christmas Eve" rule without ruining my fun for Christmas morning.

    2) I spoiled any possibility of a surprise that might have awaited my brothers when they got around to opening their packages from that aunt. We always got the same thing, even when it wasn't underwear. Any hope they might have held out for something other than underwear was dashed before they even had a chance to open their packages and see for themselves.

    3) I had more fun with a bundle of underwear than anyone should have a right to.

Brice quickly caught on and joined me on subsequent Christmas Eves in my passive-aggressive response to the stupid Christmas Eve present rule. Mom accepted defeat and allowed us to continue year after year with our idea of fun. Of course, it was all in keeping with the spirit of Christmas!

I had another aunt who was a garage sale aficionado. She had a detached three–car garage that never accommodated a car as long as I knew her. That garage was always packed wall to wall with garage sale items.

That aunt and her friends would go garage-saling just about every weekend, and they would hold a garage sale of their own once or twice a year to resell items they had picked up at bargain basement prices. I don't think my aunt made much money at it, but she would find all sorts of unique toys and eclectic items to repurpose as Christmas gifts.

We never knew what to expect from that aunt. She usually gave us something cool, something fun—*usually*. One year, Brice got a snorkel that doubled as a squirt gun. That was at a time when *Get Smart* and *Mission Impossible* were popular, and every kid wanted some normal–looking, everyday item that could double as a weapon or some sort of spy gadget.

I would have wanted a snorkel that doubled as a squirt gun, but I got golf ball soap. Yeah, I know; it's the thought that counts. But seriously? Golf ball soap? What was my aunt thinking? At that age, I had no interest in golf, and I didn't spend any more time washing with soap than I absolutely had to.

I shouldn't complain, though I think I just did. At least I got something. As for the golf ball soap, I'm over it now. Really. I am.

We had our share of pets, with two dogs and two cats. Those pets caused us a lot of trouble, as if we didn't have enough of our own. Both dogs, one male and one female, were small terrier mixes. They had the run of the place, inside and outside of the house.

At night, both dogs would crawl under the covers of our beds and sleep at our feet. They would bite us if we wiggled too much for their liking, yet we all fought over who got to have them in bed each night. We learned to sleep completely still through the night to avoid being bit. In spite of that, I generally liked the dogs.

For a short time, we had some occupants in the basement rental unit who had a dog of their own, a full–grown female Saint Bernard. The renters had jobs, and were usually gone all day, so they kept their Saint Bernard chained up in our backyard. Apparently, our male terrier mix had big aspirations, and we found him in an intimate position with the Saint Bernard on a few occasions. Fortunately, nothing came of it. I think those encounters earned our dog a trip to the vet to get neutered.

As for the cats, I never got too attached to them. One was a stray that had been hanging around the house. Brenda had been feeding it, which encouraged it to hang around all the more. Brenda begged to keep it, and of course, she got her way. We never named the stupid thing; we just called it "Kitty." I suppose you could consider that a name.

The cats also had the run of the place. At one point, a friend of Mom's asked if we could watch her family's two pet parakeets for a week while they were away on vacation. Mom agreed, without hesitation. Well, she should have hesitated long enough to think it through. Cats and birds don't mix.

After we'd had the parakeets for a few days, we were all out of the house for most of the day. We returned home to find the bird cage tipped over, lying on the floor, with a half-eaten parakeet inside. It was DOA. The other parakeet was flying hysterically around the house. We eventually trapped the live bird and placed it back in the up–righted cage.

Mom took the half-eaten parakeet to a few different pet stores in town in an effort to find a matching replacement. Surprisingly, she was able to find something close; it was even the same gender as the original. Mom introduced the counterfeit parakeet into the bird cage with the other, and the two birds got along great.

We didn't want to risk another mishap, so we all took turns guarding the bird cage until the parakeet's owners returned. Mom fessed up to her friend and apologized profusely. I doubt that the rest of that family ever knew any different.

CHAPTER 6

SCHOOL DAYS

Robert Fulghum wrote a book entitled *All I Really Need to Know I Learned in Kindergarten*. It hit #1 on the *New York Times* best seller list.[5] That's an interesting thought, but I can't say as I agree with it. (Never read the book; just goin' by the title.).

Personally, I don't recall what I knew before kindergarten, and I don't recollect what I knew immediately after. In fact, I don't even remember going to kindergarten. I'm sure I went because Mom most certainly would have wanted me out of her hair. Therefore, it's impossible for me to gauge what I learned in kindergarten.

Maybe I'm just a slow learner, but I think most of what I learned started in second grade. That's what I remember, and that's what I'm going to tell you about.

I started second grade shortly after we moved to the new place. Riverside Elementary was about four blocks from our house. My siblings and I usually walked.

At a leisurely pace, which was the pace I'd have to walk with my siblings, it would take about ten minutes. If I was running late and by myself, I could cover the distance in less than five. On most days, we would walk home for lunch, then back to school for afternoon classes.

Unless I had to take something big for show and tell, or a cumbersome project for the science fair, I wouldn't even think about having Mom drive me. Even when I wasn't feeling that great, I chose to walk. When one of my siblings needed a ride for whatever reason, I still chose to walk. To my way of thinking, having your mom drive you to school was for wimps, and I sure as heck didn't want anyone to think I was a wimp.

Riverside was home for elementary education, grades one through six, with two classrooms for each grade level. At one time, all four of us kids were attending school there, with Brett in the sixth grade, me in fifth, Brice in third, and Brenda in first.

Mom served on the PTA board and helped out with various programs like selling US Savings Bonds. Our family was fully committed to that school. After Brett and I graduated from Riverside, the boundary lines were changed. Brice and Brenda ended up completing their elementary education at A.H. Bush Elementary (formerly Whittier).

Riverside School was built in 1908. It was a two–story red brick structure with an open interior. To the front of the building was a tall flagpole around which we would gather for a ceremony every morning before school began. We'd watch as members of the staff hoisted the colors, then we'd all recite the pledge of allegiance.

The school yard had a playground with swings and a slide, a basketball court, a few tetherball poles, and a large grassy area that could be used for kickball, track and field events, tag, or whatever other games we could come up with. Inside, there was a main office on the first floor, and eight to ten classrooms around the perimeter on each level.

The school building had steam heating, piped from a central boiler in the basement to a bank of radiators in each classroom. When steam was flowing, the radiators would be scorching hot. Those hot radiators made for a source of amusement with all sorts of childish pranks, not least of which involved elimination of various body fluids.

Upon moving to the new school, I had no problem making friends. I was drawn to kids who were active and rambunctious like me. Most of my new friends were athletic, and they liked to play sports, but one of them was a kid who was not like me at all. That was Gary.

Gary didn't participate in any of the sports or other athletic activities that my other friends and I did. One day during recess, we just sort of bumped into each other and started talking. We became instant friends.

I liked Gary because he wasn't like any of my other friends. For one thing, he had a good sense of humor. He was always making me laugh. The other thing was that he was very suave and debonair with the girls. If he wasn't joking around, he was talking about girls. Gary was clearly more comfortable hanging out with girls than with boys.

That was not me. I was somewhat interested in girls, and willing to give them a try, but hanging out with girls was out of my comfort zone. So Gary invited me to tag along with him to watch and learn.

After a bit of Gary's coaching, I started to pay more attention to girls. I was beginning to get more comfortable with them.

At recess one day, Gary suggested that we let the girls have the swings. He was not just being kind or chivalrous. He had an ulterior motive. He was working on a new, as yet untested approach for getting the attention of some attractive girl he had not yet met.

With the girls on the swings, Gary's plan was to pick one out, jump from behind to grab the chains as her swing was ending its backward motion, and hitch a ride. I guess that was one way of saying, "Hello, I like you."

Without any hesitation, Gary put his plan into action. He placed himself squarely behind the swing of a pretty girl and crouched down in a ready position. He jumped at exactly the right moment, caught the chains with both hands, and hung on for the ride. Gary executed his plan to perfection. He nailed the jump, catch, and ride, and he made a positive impression on the girl. She responded with a muffled squeal and an approving smile.

While Gary was sidetracked with his new love interest, I decided to give that maneuver a try. After all, how hard could it be? Gary made it look easy. So I picked out a pretty girl, positioned myself squarely behind her swing, and crouched down in a ready position, just like Gary had done. I waited for what I thought was the right moment, and I jumped. But my attempt was a major fail.

Somehow, I badly mistimed the jump, and I was struck on the backswing by the full force of the girl, plus swing, plus chains. Dazed and confused, I staggered over to a pole that served as one of the supports for the swing set. I grabbed the pole with both hands and slowly slid down to the ground. (I only know this because Gary performed a re-enactment for me after I recovered). I was out cold.

I don't know how long I was out, but I awoke to the principal leaning over me and asking if I was okay. After coming to my senses and checking for blood (there was none), I responded that I was fine. The principal watched me walk it off before heading back to his office.

As for the object of my affection? She hung around long enough to ensure I was okay, then gave me an angry, puzzled look and stormed off with her friends. I had definitely made an impression on the girl, but it was not the kind of impression I had in mind.

Physically, I was okay, but my pride was severely wounded. I vowed to never attempt that again. That vow was easily kept because, after that incident, "hitching a ride" on swings was permanently banned from the playground at Riverside Elementary.

I was not off to a good start in relating to members of the fairer sex. I chalked up my appalling display of ineptitude on the playground to a mental lapse attributed directly to girls. I realized that I was overly distracted, perhaps even love flustered by a pretty girl, and I could not let that happen again. If I was going to make any progress with the ladies, I needed to be more cool. As Gary's apprentice, I still had a lot to learn.

After some deep conversation, Gary and I decided it was time to get more serious in our pursuit of girls, meaning we were thinking about passing notes. Gary had his eyes on a blonde, while I had mine on a brunette. And they just happened to be best friends. How perfect was that?

While I was trying to muster up the courage to pass my first note, and still trying to decide exactly what to write, I learned that Gary had jumped the gun. We were supposed to work on this project together, but he had already started passing notes to the blonde. He confessed that in one of his notes, he exposed my secret love interest in her friend, the brunette.

I'm sure Gary was just trying to be helpful, but he put me in an awkward position. With no thanks to Gary, the brunette learned of my interest in her before I was ready, and I had no idea how she felt about me. I suppose I could have sent her a note to confirm my interest, but I was hoping she would send me a note first, since my feelings for her had already been exposed.

I waited and waited, but I got nothin'. Nothin' from her, and nothin' from her friend. I had to assume that my affections for the brunette were not mutual. Rather than risk any further rejection, I chose to break off the pursuit.

After those early attempts at relationships, I was mostly ambivalent about girls. Though Gary had tried to help in that arena, I wasn't ready for it—not yet, anyway. I decided to put my focus back on sports and keep girls at arm's length for a while. If I had to choose between girls and sports, I would choose sports. Girls were just a distraction. Of course, that all changed when my hormones started to kick in a few years later.

On the subject of girls, I learned the facts of life in those early grade school years. I attribute that to a handy little pocket dictionary that Mom had quite innocently given me for Christmas. I put the dictionary in my front shirt pocket, true to form for the engineer I would eventually become, and proudly carried it off to school.

That little dictionary ended up being a huge disappointment when I found that it did not have any of the words that the boys at school asked me to look up, nor did it have any of the words my dad let loose when he was mad. That opened the door for me to inquire further as to each word's meaning. I couldn't rest until I knew.

I badgered the boys at school for answers, but they continued to string me along. It was great sport for them to poke fun at me for my naivety, but I finally coaxed it out of them. After learning all that stuff, it temporarily changed the way I looked at my parents. With them having four kids, I reckoned they must have figured all of that out themselves. I was eventually able to shrug it off and move on.

As with other kids across the nation, we were all given a series of polio vaccine shots, beginning shortly after birth. By the time I hit grade school, the medical industry had come up with a vaccine booster using a live but weakened polio virus that could be administered orally.

Once a year, we would line up at school to receive a sugar cube coated with the polio vaccine booster. I didn't have to be convinced to take it because it tasted good, and I saw what could happen if you contracted polio.

There was an older kid in the neighborhood who had been stricken with polio, and he had to walk with forearm crutches. It was hard watching him labor just to get around. I felt bad for him, and I certainly did not want to end up like him. If they would have let me, I'd have asked for two lumps of sugar; hold the coffee, please.

In those early years, my favorite subject was . . . anything but art. Being ninety-nine percent left brained, I hated art class. I could draw stick figures, stars, and simple fish—that's about it. But I loved everything else about school. I was disappointed whenever I had to miss. I was definitely an overachiever.

When my family went to Disneyland for the first time, my parents pulled me out of school for a week. Most kids would just go and have fun. I went and had fun, but I also wrote up a trip report and handed it to my teacher upon my return. I'm pretty sure that was not required.

When my third-grade class was studying the Gettysburg Address, I was consumed by it. I loved the message, and I loved the flow of the words that President Lincoln used to convey the message. I decided to commit it to memory, so one night at home after dinner, I did. I went over it and over it until I had it down.

The next day at school, I reported to my teacher, Mrs. Swanson, that I had memorized the Gettysburg Address. She had a somewhat shocked look on her face. I don't know whether that was an expression of amazement, skepticism, or bewilderment—bewildered by the strange kid standing in front of her. Whatever the case, she had me recite the address in front of the whole class.

My recitation was flawless. It didn't gain me anything, other than a sense of accomplishment and perhaps the respect of my teacher, but I was glad I did it. Looking back on that now, I'm sure that many of my classmates thought I was a dork. I suppose I was, but I didn't care. It was just something I felt compelled to do.

Other than art, most subjects came easy for me. That included spelling. When it came time for our school's spelling bee, I was brimming with confidence. I knew that I was good at it, especially compared to my friends.

My third grade class photo, 1965/66
(I'm the awkward kid in the second row wearing a bow tie)

After an administrator explained the rules, the competition began. I breezed through the first several rounds. The words were all fairly simple. As the words got harder, I watched my friends get eliminated, one by one. I knew that would happen; it was inevitable. They would be no match for me over the long haul.

After several more rounds, with the words getting even more difficult, it was down to just me and a few girls. I was not expecting that. I thought it would come down to me and a few other boys, but not girls. I know it sounds sexist, but at that point in my life, it never occurred to me that girls could be my toughest competitors, whether that be in athletics or academics.

The spelling bee continued. After the girl standing to my left breezed through her word, I was given the word "caught." I responded,

"Cot, c-o-t, cot." I couldn't believe that I had been given such an easy word. But I soon realized something was wrong when I saw a look of disappointment on the administrator's face. Graciously, she allowed me a second chance.

The administrator corrected my misunderstanding of the version of the word, slowly articulating, "Caught, as in 'I caught a fish.'" I froze. I stammered. I stumbled. Not thinking clearly, all I could do was repeat what I had already said: "Cot, c-o-t, cot." *Bzzzzzzz!* I was eliminated.

I was dumbstruck, angry, and crushed all at the same time—dumbstruck as I tried to grasp what had just happened; angry that maybe the administrator had given me a trick word (I wanted to blame someone other than myself); and crushed as I realized that my hopes for the win were dashed. I was quietly led off the stage to a seat in the audience.

The girl who had been standing to my right spelled "caught" correctly. *Arghhhh!* I knew how to spell *that* version of the word, but for some reason, my brain froze when it mattered. The girl who had been standing to my right, the very one who breezed through a word that caused me to stumble, went on to win the spelling bee.

I learned two things that day. I learned a little humility for myself. I was not as invincible as I thought. And I learned that I needed to have a little respect for girls. They could be every bit as smart as me, and maybe even smarter. They weren't just there to act cute and look pretty.

Periodically, our school classes would get to take a field trip. One particular trip that my class took is forever burned in my memory. That was our tour of the local stockyard and slaughterhouse.

The tour began innocently enough. After arriving at the stockyard, we filed out of our bus and were led to the stockyard auction room. The auction room had a large arena in the center with a dirt floor. That's where the stock would be brought in for show. There were metal stands around the perimeter of the arena where bidders and visitors would sit.

Bidding on a young heifer was in progress as we were getting seated. We got to hear a real, bona fide auctioneer do his thing. We couldn't understand what he was saying, but it was fun listening to the rhythm of his calls, as ranchers, meat processors, and other prospective buyers were making their bids.

After watching a few transactions, we left the auction room and followed along with an older cow that had just been sold for slaughter. I don't know that any of my classmates really understood what that meant. I certainly didn't, and I wasn't prepared for what would happen next.

We were led into another building that was filled with machinery. It had a dirt floor, though most of the machines were mounted on concrete pads. Looking up, I saw several pairs of long chains on pulleys. The chains were suspended from cranes that moved along overhead rails.

There was a low, constant drone of industrial fans that were used to keep the room at an uncomfortably low temperature. Workers were busy everywhere, yelling to be heard over the sounds of machinery and fans. The yelling only added to the noise. It was difficult to hear anything in there.

We formed a circle around the cow we had followed into this building. Our tour guide was talking, and probably trying to prepare us for what we were about to see, but I couldn't hear anything he was saying.

I watched a worker approach the cow and put something that looked like a handgun to its head. The cow instantly dropped, hitting the ground with a resounding thud.

Before it had even hit the ground, workers were lowering a chain directly over the top of it. They wasted no time securing the cow's hind legs to hooks on the end of the chains and hoisting the cow up. The motionless cow was lifted upside-down to where its nose was about head level to me and my classmates.

Another worker reached across the cow's neck and quickly slit its throat. He was good at what he did because I don't remember seeing a knife or any other type of cutting tool. I'm sure he used something, but he was probably being discreet about it in front of us kids.

Once the cow's throat was slit, I distinctly remember watching blood pour onto the dirt floor, with red specks splattering onto my white Converse tennis shoes. I stood there, aghast, trying to process what I had just witnessed. I think we were all stunned. Before any of us kids had time to puke or pass out, our tour guide quickly whisked us away.

Everything else about that tour was a blur for me until we came to the last stop. We filed into a large room that had been set up to display some of the products manufactured there.

I noticed a pile of tan leather gloves on a table on one side of the room. On the other side was a conveyor belt, with hot dogs rolling off, one after another. Our guide offered us a free sample. I graciously accepted and thanked the guide for the tour.

As I headed for the bus, I wolfed down that hot dog as if I hadn't eaten for days. Given what I had just witnessed, you'd think I would have no appetite for a hot dog, or any other beef product, at least not until I could clear my mind. But somehow, I was able to disassociate those sumptuous hot dogs from the image of the cow in the slaughterhouse scene.

When I finished sixth grade at Riverside Elementary, there was no fanfare. I don't recall any kind of ceremony or celebration like many schools hold for grade school graduates nowadays. My time there was just done.

As a sixth grader, it was nice being on the top rung while it lasted, but I didn't have any nostalgic thoughts about leaving. Whatever thoughts I had about school would have been focused on the next thing. Sadly, Riverside elementary was destroyed by fire in 1975. That was long after I left, so I cannot be implicated in the crime!

The next thing would be Central Junior High. All of my classmates would be joining me there that next fall for the start of our seventh–grade year, where we'd be back on the bottom rung.

CHAPTER 7

FIGHTIN' WAYS

One of the greatest and perhaps most notorious mixed martial arts fighters in recent times is Conor McGregor, ultimate fighting champion in multiple weight classes (featherweight, lightweight, and welterweight). He was quoted as saying, "I work hard and fight easy." I can relate to that, though for me as a youth, it was *play* hard and fight easy.

As an adult, I am more likely to walk away from a fight than to engage, but as a kid, I wouldn't think of walking away. Fighting was a way of life. It became second nature for me. But I learned from it; it helped to shape me and make me who I am.

Dad picked up some boxing gloves for Brett and me when we were fairly young. From his own experiences, Dad knew that we'd get into a few spats in our time, and he wanted us to be prepared.

Fighting had been a big part of Dad's life, as a kid and as an adult, both in the streets and in a ring. Dad knew his way around the ring, and he had won his share of bouts. All of that experience made him a good coach.

Dad boxing in high school, circa 1950
(That's Dad on the left, unknown opponent on the right)

Dad taught Brett and me to box—how to keep up our guard, how to lead with jabs, and how to wait for opportunities for a roundhouse punch or a swift uppercut. Our boxing lessons started with some individual coaching.

When Dad decided we were ready, he put Brett and me together as sparring partners, coaching us through our bouts. I don't think Brett really cared much for boxing, but I rather enjoyed it. I liked the adrenaline rush I felt as we touched gloves to signal the start of a bout.

Boxing combined athleticism with competition, and I was all about both. The challenge was not just to hit my opponent more than he hit me, but to make my hits count, and to make his hits not. I learned to hit accurately, to hit hard, and to work my way inside, especially when my opponent was bigger than me, which was the case in my early bouts with Brett.

Besides teaching the mechanics of boxing, Dad taught us how to think before getting into a fight. His main points were: you don't go looking for a fight, you don't run away from a fight, and when you fight, you fight to win.

Mom tried to argue the point that you just don't fight, but then she didn't really know boys. Dad knew boys. He knew that we would fight; at one time or another, we would fight.

We had our share of bullies at Riverside Elementary. I vividly recall coming home one day in my first year there as a second grader and Brett telling me about a gang of older boys at school who were bullying other kids. Their bullying included an act they referred to as pantsing, which involved dogpiling on an innocent victim and removing his pants.

My first thought was that these bullies were idiots. They were referring to this dehumanizing act as pantsing, when what they were actually doing was de-pantsing.

I would not accept their terminology. Even at that early stage in my life, I strongly believed that words mattered. Furthermore, it made no sense to me as to why they would even do such a thing. It would serve no purpose, other than to expose the victim (literally) and completely embarrass him.

As a lowerclassman, I was concerned that that could happen to me. I knew that I wouldn't be able to fight off a whole gang of upperclassmen, but I was bound and determined that I would not be a victim.

When the opportunity presented itself, I had Brett point out to me the members of this gang. They were easy to spot, as they usually hung out at the far end of the school lot. There, they could have their way with a victim before the teachers on recess duty could arrive in time to stop it.

I remember thinking that those guys were really big, and I had every intention of avoiding them.

Later that year, on a rainy fall day, I was walking home by myself after school. Out of the corner of my eye, I saw one of these gang members off to my right. He was walking along the sidewalk on the other the street but headed in the same general direction as me.

This kid was probably a fifth or sixth grader, about three or four years older than me, and definitely a lot bigger than me. When his eyes caught mine, I could sense him sizing me up. I have every reason to believe that he was preparing to de-pants me.

The bully moved out into the street, angling toward me as I continued walking straight ahead. I tried to ignore him as best I could, hoping that he would just leave me alone. But the chances of that happening seemed to diminish with every step we both took. Judging from our trajectories, I could see that our paths would soon cross.

As the bully was closing in, I noticed a large mud puddle just ahead that we would be approaching from opposite sides. I didn't want to fight, but I learned from Dad to not run away from it. And even if I did try to run, I figured the bully could easily catch me, given his much longer legs.

I thought of another option that might have made Mom proud, where I just wouldn't fight. Maybe he'd leave me alone if I were to lie down and play possum. But I figured even a dead possum could lose its pants if it was wearing any (and I was). I dismissed that thought out of hand.

I decided my best option was to take the offensive. Since the bully was alone, without his buddies there to join in, I figured I at least had a fighting chance. So when he got within range, I used the instep of my left foot to send a wall of water from the puddle in his general direction.

Score! I covered him head to toe with cold, muddy water. And *then* I took off running. I thought I might be able to evade him since I had hit my mark, and I got a good jump on him.

The bully was not expecting my strike–first approach. He may have been expecting something more like the possum approach. Initially, he was a little stunned by the cold water, and he seemed to freeze in place. But he quickly recovered and tore off after me.

The bully was faster than I expected, and he eventually caught up with me. As he approached, I stopped and turned around to give him a fight.

I ended up with a black eye, but I didn't lose my pants! I may have got the worst end of that deal, but I sent a message that I wasn't going down without a fight. I can't say whether it was that or just dumb luck, but that bully and his gang never messed with me again.

About midway through grade school, a few of us boys started a fight club, of sorts. It was intended to be a wrestling club, but when one of the contestants would get a little too rough (and that happened all too often), the wrestling match would degrade into a fist fight. Whether it was wrestling or fighting, it was all the same to me.

Our wrestling/fighting matches made for an entertaining and exhilarating recess activity. I participated in more than my share of matches, and I was able to hold my own, thanks in part to the training I received from Dad.

I wish I could say that I did as well in following Dad's advice to not go looking for a fight, but it didn't always work that way. I completely failed on one notable occasion, when I picked a fight with a classmate for no good reason. Fighting within the club was okay, at least to my way of thinking. In those fights, all contestants were willing. But fighting outside of the club was a separate matter, especially with an unwilling contestant (i.e., a victim).

After our club matches had been going for a while, some of the kids in the club decided to pick a fight with a classmate. I'll call him Charlie, who wonders, "Why is everybody always pickin' on me?"[6]

Charlie was of average height with a slim build, mild-mannered and soft-spoken. He was one of the few kids in our class who regularly wore glasses. Charlie was not part of the fight club, and he was certainly not the kind of kid who would go looking for a fight.

I'm not sure why some of the kids in the club decided to pick on Charlie. It may be that they were getting bored with the club flights because we had an established pecking order based on the results of previous matches, and there was not much room for movement in that order, up or down. Charlie may have represented a new challenge to them.

Every other day or so, a different kid from our club would pick a fight with Charlie. Even for the kids at the bottom of the pecking order, those fights were no contest. It should have ended when it became clear that fighting with Charlie would be punching down. But it didn't; not right away. The wheels had been set in motion, and everyone else in the club felt like they had to have their go at Charlie. I'm not proud of the fact that that included me.

I picked a fight with Charlie one morning while we were waiting for school to start. Before we really got into it, the principal broke it up. He went back to his office and returned with two pair of boxing gloves. He took us aside and asked us to put them on if we wished to continue. Of course I wished to continue. I was very comfortable in a pair of boxing gloves, and I was ready to go. Charlie, on the other hand, wanted no part of it. He immediately declined.

The principal scolded us for fighting, told us something about trying to work out our disagreements verbally rather than physically, had us shake hands, and sent us off to class. I felt bad for Charlie. That scolding should have been for me, alone, not for him.

Charlie was smart in not wanting to fight. If he had agreed to fight, he would have ended up fighting (and losing to) every single kid in our club before it was over. Fortunately, I think that did end it for Charlie. After that, nobody else from our club picked a fight with him.

In hindsight, I was glad Charlie didn't want to put on those gloves. I would have won handily, and I would have been labeled a bully by

Charlie and a lot of my other classmates. That was not what I wanted. I recoiled at the very thought of being lumped together with those gang members who I had so feared as a second grader.

Reflecting on that experience, I realized the wisdom of dad's advice for me to not go looking for a fight. In the bigger picture, winning that fight would have meant losing.

The principal eventually put a stop to our fight club, though I think it would have died a natural death, anyway. For one thing, we were all beginning to get bored with it. And secondly, as the fights were getting more violent and indiscriminate, we were starting to lose friends among our classmates. Not many of them cared to watch. They didn't want to see us beat up on each other or anyone else who got in our way.

After fight club, we moved on. It wasn't like we started a chess club or a French poetry club or anything else of a more genteel nature. We just scaled it back a notch and moved on to other physical activities of a less rough and aggressive nature; activities like dodge ball, tackle football, and full contact tag.

On one warm, spring day, after we'd been in the neighborhood three or four years, a friend and I decided to take our younger brothers to the playground at Highland Park. My friend's younger brother, Kent was about the same age as Brice. Kent and Brice were good friends, and I considered Kent my little buddy, too.

After we'd been playing at the park for a while, we were resting on the merry-go-round, discussing the mysteries of the universe or something equally perplexing. As we were talking, we observed a tall, lanky kid with very long, curly hair, about 40 yards off. I'll call this kid Slim, as in someone *"you don't mess around with"*.[7]

I'd never seen Slim before, but he was clearly much bigger and older than any of us. He was just casually passing through the park, paying us no attention. That is until Kent asked, "Is that a boy or a girl?" in a voice loud enough for Slim to hear.

Kent didn't mean to be disrespectful; he was just curious. Honestly, I wasn't sure myself, when I first saw Slim, so I understood why Kent would ask that question. I'm sure that he didn't intend for Slim to hear him. Kent just had a loud voice. Regardless, that stopped Slim dead in his tracks.

Slim hollered back, "What did you just say?" as he started heading our direction.

By then, it was clear to all of us that Slim was no girl. Kent didn't know when to shut up. He replied, "I was just asking if you were a boy or a girl."

Slim came over and started slapping Kent around. With each slap, Kent just laughed, the kind of nervous laugh you have when you don't know how else to respond. The more Slim slapped Kent, the more Kent laughed. We all started to laugh because of the way Kent was standing up to Slim. That just made it worse. Slim became enraged.

Slim then angrily threatened, "I'll beat the snot out of the next person who laughs."

I wasn't sure exactly what to do, but I figured Kent wouldn't let it go. He'd probably laugh again and end up getting beat to a pulp. I couldn't stand by and let that happen.

Before Kent had a chance to respond, I responded with my best fake laugh, "Ha, ha."

Slim immediately diverted his attention away from Kent and came after me. I stood up to fight and gave it my best shot. And just as Slim promised, he beat the snot out of me.

I ended up with a fat lip and two black eyes, but I probably saved Kent from worse. If I had it to do over, I would do everything the same, unless I could somehow muzzle Kent first.

About the time I hit junior high, I had a built a reputation as a fighter. Sure, I had lost a few bouts, but I wasn't afraid to fight, and I would not back down.

I didn't realize it at the time, but my reputation had put a mark on my back. There were kids I didn't even know who tried to pick a fight with me, and for no apparent reason. I felt a little bit like Charlie from grade school, but it was a little different for me. I knew how to fight, and I wasn't smart enough to back down.

On one occasion, a kid in the neighborhood casually mentioned on our bus ride home that he wanted to meet me at the park on Saturday morning for a fight. I'll call this kid Curly because he had crazy curly hair. It was sort of like a showdown at high noon, only it was fisticuffs at 10:00 a.m. I had a little apprehension about it, as I didn't know what to expect. I wasn't afraid of a fair fight, but how could I be sure this would be a fair fight?

That Saturday morning, I got up early as usual, ate breakfast, and went alone to the park at the appointed time. As I half expected, Curly was not alone. He had his two cousins with him. They were both bigger and older than me.

As Curly and I started to fight, it became clear that his cousins were not just there to encourage him. And I don't think they were just there to coach him, either. I'm fairly certain that they were there to take over, if necessary.

I was having no trouble with Curly. He was slow, and he didn't have much arm strength. But I was not so sure about his cousins. At best, I'd have to face them one at a time after I was done with Curly. At worst . . . well, I didn't even have to go there. I decided to throw the fight.

When Curly landed a kick a little close to my developing manhood, I feigned a direct hit and doubled over. After "regaining my strength," I conceded the fight to him. We shook hands and parted ways. The cousins walked away happy that their boy had prevailed, but I think Curly was just happy to walk away.

I could have easily won that fight; I knew it, and Curly knew it. From that point on, he would go out of his way to avoid me. He wanted no part in a rematch without his cousins around.

I didn't mind throwing that fight. It may have hurt my pride a little in the short term, but in the long term it didn't really cost me a thing. In fact, I think I came out ahead on the deal. For one, I probably saved my skin by not having to face Curly's cousins. And for another, I no longer had a target on my back.

My fighting days ended right where they started . . . with my older brother Brett. For the most part, he and I got along as best we could. Though he was my Irish twin, and we occupied space in the same household, we lived in two different worlds. We mostly just stayed out of each other's way. We had a few minor skirmishes from time to time, but most of our disputes amounted to little more than yelling and thumping of chests.

Brett and I sort of took the same approach as the US and USSR during the cold war, formally known as Mutually Assured Destruction (MAD). The idea was that neither country would attack the other (specifically, with nuclear weapons), knowing that their own country would be destroyed in the process.

For Brett and me, that MAD approach kept us at an uneasy peace until one day in our high school years when a dispute arose over use of the family car. That dispute escalated to the point that our cold war went hot. It ended in a full—on, knock—down, drag—out fist fight. We more or less fought to a draw.

Brett and I showed up at church the next morning with bruised and battered faces. We did our best to put on a good front as we joined the congregation in singing hymns of love, joy, and peace. After that incident, Brett and I reverted to a policy of détente. Over the years, we've had many more arguments and differences of opinion, but we've never waged another hot war.

Though we had our differences, I had to admire Brett for his courage of conviction. That fight in high school never proved anything, other than the fact that we were big enough, strong enough, and skilled enough at fighting to put the hurt on each other. And at the end of the day, Brett was standing up for what was right. I was in the wrong. And I knew it.

By the way, that wasn't the first time Brett put his neck on the line for his convictions. He stood up to Dad a few times earlier in life when Dad was physically abusive with Mom, while Brice and I were cowering under our beds. Dad also knew he was in the wrong, and he ended up backing down. I think he respected Brett for taking a stand.

One lesson I learned from my fighting days is that, win or lose, I'd almost always come away feeling bad. When I'd win a fight, I'd have an initial feeling of euphoria as I basked in the glow of my triumph. But as the adrenaline rush would begin to dissipate, I'd start to feel a little sympathy for my opponent. There's that little spark of compassion showing through.

The exception was winning a fight with a bully. In that situation, I wouldn't feel bad at all. The bully got what he deserved, and he would receive no mercy or sympathy from me.

When I'd lose a fight, I had plenty of reasons to come away feeling bad. Whether it was from a black eye, a fat lip, or a bruised ego, it would hurt, just the same. And it would all take time to heal.

My takeaway from all that is that, if I had to choose, I'd still choose to win. I'd just choose to be a little smarter about fighting to begin with.

That leads to the advice I would offer to anyone reading. I wouldn't pass along the exact advice I got from Dad *or* Mom, though I think there's value in both. Rather, I believe the best advice involves a combination of the two. My advice would be: "Do everything you can to avoid a fight, but if you have to fight, fight to win."

I would love to go back and give this advice to my younger self. It may not have helped me to avoid a few black eyes (some things are always worth fighting for), but I think it would have saved me a lot of trouble and heartache. And who knows whether or not this advice would have been well received. My younger self was a pretty hard–headed kid.

CHAPTER 8

THE SHACK
(BROKEN RULES PART I)

Yogi Berra, the American baseball great and humorist, was famously quoted as saying, "When you come to a fork in the road, take it."[8] Well, that was my philosophy in the new 'hood. I wanted to explore, and I didn't necessarily care in what direction. For me, everything outside of the house was a new frontier, waiting to be tamed. This chapter includes a compilation of several forks I took along the roads of exploration.

Most of my experiences in the new 'hood were shared with my little sidekick, Brice. Despite our age difference, he followed me step for step over, under, around, and into most places I was able to get—including into trouble.

At one time, Mom was so angry with us (mostly me) for whatever infraction we may or may not have committed that she accused me of creating a little Frankenstein's monster. I preferred to think of us more as Lewis and Clark on our best days, or perhaps Butch Cassidy and the Sundance Kid on our worst. But Dr. Frankenstein and his monster? Please!

Brice had a mind of his own, and he joined me because that is what he wanted to do. And no matter what label you want to apply, I think he turned out pretty good. All of that to say that when I refer to *we* and *us* in relating my childhood explorations and activities, I am usually referring to Brice and me. I cannot implicate Brett or Brenda in any of those shenanigans.

Brice may not *want* to be implicated, but he was there. Whether he was there as Lt. William Clark or the Sundance Kid, as God is my witness, he was there!

For the first year or so after our move, I mostly just went to school and stayed close to home. I played a lot of indoor board games with my siblings and made up a few of my own. I was never into playing trucks or playing roles that required a lot of imagination.

When I'd go to a friend's house and he'd want to play trucks, I would try to oblige him, but I could only take it for so long. In short order, I'd bail on the toy trucks and head straight for the swing set. If there was no swing set, I'd find a ball to kick or throw. I much preferred activities and games that were more physical.

As a birthday gift, someone had given me a package of plastic green and tan army men. Brice and I played with them quite a bit, but not as you might expect. There was no hollering out commands to soldiers positioning for a fight, no sounding out the rapid fire of machine guns and explosions of mortar shells, no narration of various battle engagements. No, our game pitted us against the toy army men.

Initially, we would set the army men up on wood blocks and shoot them down with homemade rubber band guns. It was not a game of competition. Rather, it was a team effort for us to fire until all of the men were down. When we eventually tired of using rubber band guns to engage the enemy from the ground, we took the army men outside to engage them from the air.

After some experimentation with various materials, we learned that the plastic used for bread sacks would behave like napalm when wrapped around the end of a stick and lit on fire. So we set up the army men on the driveway and firebombed them. That was a ton of fun, but it was short-lived. When enough of the army men got melted to the point that they could no longer stand, the fun was over.

As we all began to get comfortable in our new surroundings, Mom eventually let us venture out. Overall, the neighborhood seemed fairly safe.

Before turning us loose, Mom made clear two rules that we absolutely had to follow if we wanted to go out and explore on our own. These were the kind of rules that if you broke them, you would be grounded for life.

Rule #1: Never play around the shack and wood piles next door.

Rule #2: See Chapter 9.

I considered Rule #1 to be overly protective, and I was not about to follow it. I would just have to be careful to not get caught. Being grounded for life could be a long time, depending on how far I pressed my luck (i.e., my life could be much shorter than expected if things really went south).

I won't say the shack was the first place I went, but Mom's warning had just placed it high on my list.

The obvious first place to explore was our own yard. It didn't take long for us to test our physical prowess from the retaining wall on the side of the house, which involved an eight–foot jump to the ground below. That seemed pretty high at the time, but we had the luxury of a soft, grassy landing.

We learned how to jump and roll with the landing to minimize impact. When we played tag with other kids, the retaining wall was an easy escape route for us experienced jumpers. Most kids would not intentionally make that jump.

On a few occasions, some random kid would inadvertently go off the wall. More often than not, those inadvertent "falls" involved a bit of encouragement from someone else's hand or foot.

Nobody ever got seriously hurt, but Mom didn't want to press her luck. She tried putting a stop to our jumping by planting a flower garden just below the retaining wall. That only made it more of a challenge, as it provided an obstacle for us to clear. It did reduce the number of inadvertent "falls", though.

We'd get in trouble if *anyone* landed in the flower garden. And somehow, Mom could always tell when that happened. I suspect the broken stems and flattened petals may have clued her in.

From time to time, we set up other games and obstacles in the backyard. One evening as the family was gathered to watch a show on television, one of our dogs jumped up onto a card table that Mom was using for snacks. Everyone was praising the little mutt, making a huge fuss over *his* physical prowess.

I must have felt the need for some of that attention, so I declared that I could not only jump on the card table; I could jump over it. Dad immediately called me out on that. He challenged me to put my money where my mouth was.

The bet was one dollar. Dad added a stipulation was that if I broke the table, I'd have to pay for a new one. Somewhat reluctantly, I agreed. I was fairly confident I could do it, but I wasn't so sure of how the table might fare. I figured that if I failed, I could probably scrape together a dollar for losing the bet, but there was no way I could cover the cost of a new card table.

Dad gave me one day to practice. I would have to prove myself when he got home from work the next day.

Thanks to whoever built our retaining wall, I was getting to be fairly good at jumping. But this was different. I wouldn't be jumping down and over; I'd be jumping up and over. And I'd be fighting gravity all the way up.

I was glad to have a day to practice. I set up the card table in the backyard, ensuring a location where I would have plenty of runway in front and a soft landing on the other side. It was a standard folding card table; the dimensions would have been about thirty inches in height, and thirty-six by thirty-six inches square.

On my first attempt, I took a good lead–up run, long enough to hit my stride. At the last possible moment, just as I reached the table, I pulled up and stopped. Where was my confidence?

My second attempt was a repeat of the first. This was looking to be a lot harder than I thought. In the back of my mind, I was thinking about breaking the table and being forever enslaved, or at least until I could come up with the money for a new one.

I was eventually able to put that out of my mind; if it happens, it happens. I took a good lead–up run for a third attempt. As I approached the point of no return, I let my feet leave the ground, and cleared the table with room to spare.

I made several more successful jumps before ending my practice session. I needed to save a little strength in my legs for the actual event.

When Dad got home and saw the smile on my face, he must have known that he had already lost the bet. Making the jump with Dad there to witness was just a formality. So I did it, once again clearing the table with room to spare.

Dad didn't say a word, but I could tell by the glimmer in his eyes that he was impressed. He took the billfold out of his back pocket, and agonizingly pried a dollar bill from its fold. He then slowly reached over to hand it to me, making it look like it was the last dollar he had to his name.

In hindsight, I think Dad was baiting me. And it worked. I felt sorry for him, and I was compelled to give him an out. I told Dad that if he could also jump over the table, I would give his dollar back.

I really wasn't sure Dad could do it. He had a height advantage over me, but he also had a weight disadvantage. At the time, Dad was in decent shape from playing softball, but that was somewhat offset by a big ol' beer belly.

Like son, like father, Dad took a few practice runs up to the table and stopped short. Then he went for it. If he failed, the card table would have been kaput for sure, and I'd better not be held responsible for that.

Surprisingly, Dad made it. He didn't make it look easy, but he made it. I was happy to give Dad his dollar back. I probably would have wasted it on candy at Russ's Market anyway. Dad and I were both able to walk away from that challenge with our pride intact. And the card table came away unscathed.

Brice and I played all sorts of games in our backyard. Invariably, a ball would end up in the next door neighbor's backyard.

There was a four–foot high chain–link fence separating our backyard from the neighbor's. The fence had a latching gate which provided access between. That would have made it easy to retrieve overthrown objects, if not for Caesar.

Caesar was a large, lonely male English bulldog. Anything or anyone entering his domain became the object of his affections. Caesar could easily overpower most grade schoolers, and it would be a struggle to get away without being covered with some sort of slime.

As an aside, I didn't connect the slime to what I had previously learned from my grade school pocket dictionary experience until years later.

Anyway, we found that our best chance for a successful retrieval was to have one kid distract Caesar from our side of the fence, while another hopped the fence and scrambled for the ball.

The probability of getting back unmolested and unslimed was low, but molested or unmolested, slimed or unslimed, we always managed to get the kid and the ball back. It was just annoying enough that we tried really hard to avoid hitting, kicking, or throwing any object of value into the neighbor's backyard.

One night we were awakened to the sounds of sirens and people screaming. We rushed outside to see our next–door neighbor's house going up in flames. The street was filled with fire trucks and other emergency vehicles. There were countless firemen working to control the flames and to keep the fire from spreading to adjacent homes, including ours.

Mom opened our home to the firemen and other first responders, providing them with food, water, and coffee as they worked through the night. They were able to contain the fire, but despite their efforts, our neighbor's house was a total loss.

We were heartbroken for our neighbors. They ended up moving away, and we were sad to see them go. However, there was a silver lining beneath that black cloud of smoke that hung over the smoldering embers next door. When our neighbors moved away, Caesar went with them!

Another backyard game we enjoyed was Frisbee, but we played it before any of us knew what a Frisbee was. Apparently, the first official Frisbee was manufactured by the Wham-O company in 1957, and its popularity quickly spread in the sixties and seventies. We had no idea that was a thing.

We invented our own game of Frisbee, using a medium–sized cymbal from my drum set (I took up drums after dumping the accordion). Throwing the cymbal Frisbee was a lot of fun. The cymbal had great aerodynamics, and it could really soar.

Catching the cymbal was an entirely separate matter. We quickly learned that catching it straight on could result in injuries that would usually require some attention.

On those few occasions when the cymbal sailed over our heads and into the neighbor's yard, it would often end up embedded a few inches into the sod on the side of their hill. We found that a better, less painful approach to catching the cymbal was to reach out and grab it from the side as it was flying by. We eventually replaced the cymbal with a real plastic Frisbee and saved ourselves a few additional scars.

At times, our backyard became a shooting range for BB guns, arrows, and darts. Dad taught us the basics of firearm safety, so we were usually pretty careful to not shoot or throw when someone was downrange.

On one occasion, however, our safety training failed us, and Brice got hit in the eye with a dart. Nobody knows exactly how that happened. One minute we were gathering darts; the next minute—*zing*—and there's this dart hanging off Brice's eyelid.

I don't recall Brice even crying. It must have at least stung a little, but he may have been in shock, trying to figure out what had just happened. Since the dart didn't penetrate the eyelid, it was "No harm, no foul." That incident *did* instill in us a little more respect for dart safety.

Mom planted a vegetable garden in our backyard. We helped out with the watering and the weeding. Other than that, the garden was her baby.

Whether Mom intended it or not, her garden provided us with a lot of nutritional snacks on days that we would spend most of our time outside. It was a lot easier to pull up a carrot or snap off some peas for a quick snack than to go back to the house for something that would inevitably be less healthy (like a frozen Hostess pastry).

Other gardens in the neighborhood seemed fair game when we ventured beyond our backyard. Nobody ever got after us for stealing from their gardens. It wouldn't surprise me if the neighborhood moms were all in cahoots on that. Planting vegetable gardens throughout the neighborhood would have been an easy way to ensure their kids were all snacking right.

As we began to lose interest in the backyard, we looked for new excitement in the alleyway and the vacant lot next door.

I had gained an interest in rocks and fossils from my Grandpa Davis, and I spent countless hours looking for fossils among the gravel stones in the alleyway. Dad assured me that I wouldn't find any fossils there. That only encouraged me in my search.

After what probably amounted to several weeks of looking, I actually found one. When I showed it to Dad, he shrugged it off, and seemed a little annoyed. I don't know whether he was annoyed that I had wasted so much time, or that I had worked so hard to prove him wrong. Either way, I didn't care. I thought it was time well spent; however, after proving my point, I had no desire to search for any more fossils.

On another occasion, I came upon a whole pile of various polished stones in the vacant lot next door. It was an amazing find, which included agates, tiger eyes, map rocks (crazy lace agate), and Petoskey stones, to name a few.

Oddly enough, those were just the types of stones my grandpa had in his collection. When I showed Mom my find, she confessed that Grandpa had given her part of his collection, and she didn't want them. She didn't know what to do with them, so she tossed them in the vacant lot.

I'll never know why Mom tossed the stones there. It could be that she did it knowing I would find them, and that it would bring me great joy. And it did. However, my great joy was greatly diminished in knowing how the stones got there.

Another find from the vacant lot came from inside the forbidden shack. To get to the shack, we had to climb over piles of loose boards, being careful to avoid stepping on any exposed nails.

We were clearly breaking the first of Mom's two absolute rules, but we had to do it. We were drawn to the shack like moths to a flame.

As we entered the shack, we disturbed a colony of bats. We had to duck as a few of them made their escape over our heads and out the door that we had just propped open.

Inside the shack, it was dark and damp, and smelled of mildew. Not much was in there, other than cobwebs, more piles of wood, and rodent droppings on top of rodent droppings.

In the shadows, we were able to make out a box that was tucked away in one corner, somewhat obscured by a stack of wood. That got our attention. We had to examine its contents to see what kind of treasures might await us.

As we went to lift the box, we found it to be heavier than expected. With some effort, we moved it toward the door where the lighting was a little better.

When we opened the box, we could see that the treasure inside was a stack of girlie magazines and two bottles of liquor. Apparently, this contraband had been stashed away by someone whose wife or mother would not have wanted it in their house. We put the box back where we found it and hightailed it out of there.

We were young enough to not have much interest in the magazines or the liquor, and we didn't want whoever put it there to know that we had discovered it. When we got back home, we told Mom of our discovery, even though we were implicating ourselves in our disobedience.

Surprisingly, Mom didn't ground us for life. She didn't even get mad. It could be that she was so happy with us for doing the right thing (telling her about the stash) that she forgot we were doing the wrong thing when we found it. Or more likely, she was distracted thinking about who might have put the stash there, and whether they might be back to look for it.

I don't know whatever became of that contraband, but it wasn't there on our next visit. In fact, we never came across anything like that in the shack again. Too bad for the guy whose secret hideaway was blown!

As a side note, I did eventually step on a nail while climbing over the wood piles in my explorations of the shack. My foot and leg began to stiffen up, and I realized I couldn't just rub a little dirt on it to make it go away. I ended up in the ER with tetanus and had to get a shot to treat it.

Mom was proven right. She was one for one with her rules that we absolutely should have followed.

Next on our radar was Angels ballpark, but before we went there you might say it came to us. With our property located just on the other side of the fence from center right field, we'd get an occasional home–run ball in our backyard.

Some of the neighbor kids were always looking to shag home–run balls, and they'd go out of their way to find them. But oftentimes Dad was also on the lookout. He ran off more than one kid who dared step foot in our yard in their quest. I don't know which he enjoyed more: startling the trespassers or collecting the balls. In any event, Brice and I had an ample supply of practice balls before we ever started playing the game.

Another exciting aspect of having the stadium in our backyard was when the circus came to town. The Shrine Circus came every year while we lived there. They would set up the big tent inside the baseball stadium, and we could see part of the show, especially the high wire acts, from our kitchen window.

The lions, tigers, monkeys, elephants, and other exotic animals were kept in cages outside the stadium, just up the alley and around the corner from our house. We would often take the time to go see the animals, without having to pay to see the circus.

Occasionally, one of our dogs would drag home a fresh chunk of elephant poop as a souvenir. The chunk of poop was about half as big as the dog. It would last him a few weeks before it got dry enough for him to lose interest.

Venturing a little farther from home, Brice and I made our way to the city park. Just past the small baseball field, we locked eyes on some ginormous pine trees.

We had never seen trees so tall. They seemed to draw us in. We loved to climb, and those trees looked like they were made for climbing. It was a match made in heaven. We had an apple tree in our backyard that we liked to climb, but it could only take us so high. Those pine trees would literally take us to new heights.

As we got a little closer, it was clear to see that those trees had been climbed before. That only encouraged us. So up we went.

We were soon well above the height of our apple tree. With each additional step, we set a new record high.

The climbing was easy, but it was also a little scary. If we fell, we would probably not survive. That made it all the more thrilling. Climbing those trees became our new passion.

Then came the day when, blindly reaching my hand over the next higher branch, I felt something unexpected and squishy. Upon close inspection, using three of my five senses and having ruled out taste as an option, I concluded that it was human feces. Are you kidding me? Other than birds and squirrels, who in the world would poop in the tree?

With the utmost urgency, I retreated down the tree and quickly rinsed my hands in the creek. Brice had the same experience on a separate occasion.

Several weeks later, on another trip to the park, we saw some kids preparing to climb those same trees. We warned them about the possibility of a poop encounter, but they said they had been there before and were aware of it. They blamed the Duttons for it. (Those were the kids we were told to avoid.)

I'm not sure how or why they would have known that the Duttons did it, but we figured it must have been true because they said so. After that experience, we still loved to climb those trees, but the honeymoon was over.

Highland Park came alive in the summer, with all sorts of activities for kids. There were arts and crafts classes at the log hut (educational building), lessons at the tennis courts, and always games at the baseball field.

That first summer, Mom enrolled us boys in tennis lessons. I learned the basics of the game, and I enjoyed it, but it didn't hold my interest.

The next summer, against my wishes, Mom enrolled us in the arts and crafts classes. I'm sure she enjoyed getting all of us out of the house and having some time to herself. And it was probably comforting for her to know that we were doing something "constructive." But to me, it was just plain torture.

As I suffered through each session, my attention was more and more drawn to the other end of the park, where there was always a baseball game in progress. My mind easily drifted from the art project to baseball and to one day being able to play.

CHAPTER 9

THE RIVER
(BROKEN RULES PART II)

"We have an unknown distance yet to run, an unknown river to explore. What falls there are, we know not; what rocks beset the channel, we know not; what walls ride over the river, we know not. Ah, well! We may conjecture many things."[9] These were the words of John Wesley Powell as he was preparing his descent into the Grand Canyon.[9] These could just as easily have been my words as I was preparing to explore the Snake River.

As a kid, the Snake River seemed every bit as foreboding to me as the Grand Canyon must have seemed to John Wesley Powell. You couldn't live in my neighborhood without having some awareness of the Snake River and the dangers it posed. With apologies to Mom, who would never have condoned my many river exploits, I present this chapter, where the river runs through my memoirs.

Remember those two rules Mom insisted we follow before turning us loose to explore on our own? The ones that, if we broke them, we'd be grounded for life? I talked about Rule #1 in Chapter 8. Here's the other:

Rule #2: "Never go near the river!"

The fact that Mom told us to never go near the river made it all the more tempting. In fact, it put the river near the top of the places we had to explore. It took Brice and me a while to get there, though, because it was such a long way from home, at least by our standard of measure. And there were so many other places to explore along the way.

Besides the distance being a factor, we also had an innate sense of caution about the river. Though we'd been taking swim lessons at the city pool, and had conquered the deep end, we weren't very confident of our abilities in open water. It was one thing to jump into a pool where we knew the depth and could see the bottom. It was quite another to plunge into a lake or river where the depth was unknown and the water too murky to make out the bottom.

A few years after the move, having explored just about everything worth exploring close to home, we were more than ready to make our way to the river. By then, we had a few years of swim lessons under our string ties. We also had a little experience in open water, having spent some time water skiing and swimming in lakes during a number of family outings. ˒

With a large dose of unwarranted confidence, Brice and I felt that we were ready for the big time . . . "Snake River, here we come!"

In preparation for our river swim, we put on our swim trunks, stepped into our flip-flops, grabbed our towels, and headed out the door. Summer was just around the corner, and it was turning out to be a beautiful spring afternoon.

We hadn't gone far before we realized that walking much distance in flip-flops is not easy. They were uncomfortable, and they were beginning to wear blisters between our toes. I'd like to have ditched them, but my feet were too tender to walk any distance without some kind of foot covering.

We continued plodding along in our flip-flops as best we could. Getting to the river ended up taking us a lot longer than we had expected.

When we finally arrived, we could see that the river was running high, and the current was swift. There was no easy access to the river from our closest approach on the east side. The riverbank in that area was steep and marshy.

On the west side of the river, directly across from where we were standing, the access looked a little easier. In fact, there was a section of bank on that side that looked like a boat launch, with a nice, gradual slope from the shore into the river.

We had to check it out. Our best approach to get there was over a bridge, just a few hundred yards upstream from our location. That was our first real view of the Johns Hole Bridge.

As we headed toward the bridge, we observed some kids gathered on the far west side. There were about a half dozen or so. One by one, they were making their way over the railing and jumping off the bridge into the river below, then swimming to shore and climbing back up from the other side.

Brice and I looked at each other with big eyes and big grins. Those kids looked to be having a ton of fun, and we wanted to get in on it. Without speaking a word, we hurried our pace to the top of the bridge, and over to the other side, flip-flops be damned.

As we approached the west side, we got a better look at the kids there. Most of them were wearing cut-offs, T-shirts, and sneakers. They ranged in age from about eight to fourteen. The oldest two, who I took to be brother and sister, seemed to be in charge.

We watched the group closely for several minutes. They had a system that apparently helped them to look out for one another. When one of them jumped, everyone else would watch and wait for him (or her) to swim safely to shore before the next one would go.

While we watched, we too kept track of the kids as they jumped and made their way to shore. As near as we could tell, every kid who jumped into the river made it safely back. The survival rate was right at about 100 percent, give or take. Those seemed like pretty good odds to us.

The river wasn't proving to be nearly as risky as Mom wanted us to believe. Even with the added danger of jumping off the bridge, it seemed fairly safe. We didn't need any more convincing. We were going to jump!

Before getting started, we thought it best to get a few details from the experts. We approached the brother and sister duo just after they had climbed back up to the bridge. They were kind enough to stop what they were doing and give us the lowdown.

The brother informed us, "The water runs deep on the far west side below the bridge, deep enough to make for a safe jump." He showed us exactly where to jump from the bridge to hit the deeper water.

Brice and I acknowledged with a simple, understanding nod.

His sister added, "Be sure to swim with the current, not against it."

Again, Brice and I acknowledged with a nod, acting as if we knew exactly what she was talking about.

She must have seen a little confusion on our faces as she went on to make it a little more clear. She pointed out the boat launch area just downstream of the bridge. "See there, where the slope from the river to the shore is more gradual? After you jump, swim downstream to that point. From there, it's also easier access back to shore."

As she was talking, I noticed her looking at our attire a little sideways and looking wryly back at her brother in some sort of nonverbal communication. After she finished instructing us on how to swim *with* the current, her brother gave us a little tutorial on the appropriate wear for bridge jumping. "I wouldn't recommend jumping off the bridge in a pair swim trunks. Cut-offs will provide for a little more protection of stuff you want to protect when you hit the water."

We understood the point. We hadn't thought about the impact of hitting the water after jumping from that height. That must be what his sister was wanting to communicate in a manner that would not embarrass us. She had her brother spell it out for us.

He continued, "And you gotta have sneakers or something for your feet other than flip-flops. You need something to keep your feet from getting cut up on rocks as you climb back to shore."

The brother and sister duo told us just about everything we needed to know for a fun and safe jumping experience. We thanked them for their time, and they rejoined their group.

Brice and I were grateful for the advice, but it was a bit of a let-down. When we first saw those kids jump, we were hoping that we could join in right away. But after getting a little education on the subject, it was clear that we had not come prepared. We were not appropriately dressed for the occasion. We thought about trying it anyway; after all, we did have Viking blood.

Ultimately, we decided against jumping (and swimming) that day. There were too many factors working against us to make it a fun and safe experience. But we would back; without question, we would be back!

At the next opportunity, Brice and I returned to the Johns Hole Bridge dressed more appropriately for jumping off the bridge and swimming in the river. We were each wearing a pair of faded cut-off jeans, an old holey T-shirt, and a pair of worn—out sneakers.

We made a lot better time getting to the river in our sneakers than we had made in our flip-flops. As we approached the bridge, we could see that no one else was there. We'd be completely on our own.

We were a little apprehensive to go it alone, but it wasn't like we'd be hitting it blind. We had received detailed instructions on the whole process, and we had witnessed several jumps. We assured ourselves that we could do this.

We made our way to the west side of the bridge, gingerly climbed over the railing, and looked down at the river. The distance from the bridge to the river was about twenty feet. That was ten to twelve feet higher than the highest springboard from which we had ever jumped at the local swimming pool.

Our courage wavered slightly (actually, our courage wavered a lot). From our vantage point there on the edge of the bridge, the view was a lot different than it was from the "safe" side of the railing. The height from which we'd be jumping looked even higher from there.

We stood there for a while, looking down, trying to get our courage up. It was a warm, sunny afternoon, but it was still spring; the water would be icy cold. We would not only be braving a record high jump, but also the cold water, and potentially dangerous currents.

Since we had already made it that far, there was no turning back. We had no choice but to jump. We just needed a little more incentive. Our Viking blood wasn't exactly cutting it at that moment. The situation called for a countdown.

With a countdown, we'd be compelled to jump at the same time. Neither of us would want to be shamed by the other for holding back. And so it went. In unison, we hollered out, "Three . . . two . . . one . . . Geronimo!" and in unison we jumped.

The shock we experienced as we plunged into the cold water was diminished by the exuberance we felt in making (and surviving) our first leap off the Johns Hole Bridge! It was a rush!

After conquering our fears to make that jump, the rest was easy. Going with the current, we had an easy swim to the boat launch area, and an almost effortless climb up to the shore. We drip dried in the warmth of the afternoon sun as we hiked back up to the bridge. Then, without hesitation, we climbed over the railing and jumped again, and again, and again.

The cold water was more noticeable on our subsequent jumps, but that didn't deter us. It really was a ton of fun. We must have made at least a dozen jumps that day.

Jumping off the bridge for the first time was more frightening than we had expected, but it was even more fun than we could have imagined. The adrenaline rush we experienced was enhanced with the knowledge that we had conquered our fears and laughed in the face of danger.

We ended up going back to the Johns Hole Bridge time and time again, and we'd bring our friends along to jump with us. Brice even went night jumping with a few of his friends.

We continued going back to jump off that bridge well into our adult lives . . . until the city permanently banned it and began fining violators. We may or may not have jumped a few times after that. I can't say one way or another because I don't know whether or not there's a statute of limitations that would have expired by now.

On our many trips to the river, we noticed an island about a quarter of a mile downstream of the Johns Hole Bridge. That was officially known as Keefer's Island. By then, we were a lot more confident of our swimming abilities, having braved the river after our many jumps off the bridge. We thought we had a good feel for the river and its currents, but our only experience was on the west side below the bridge, where the current is fairly gentle.

In reality, we didn't know the river and its currents at all. The currents farther from shore are not so forgiving. We had given some thought to swimming out to the island and back. It seemed like a nice challenge. And if the water wasn't so cold, I just may have tried it.

After I left home for college, Brice actually did try it, and thank God he made it. Over the years several people have drowned trying. And like Brice and I, most of them were good swimmers.

Somewhere along the way, we learned from some neighbor kids that there were depressions or cave–like structures behind some of the large boulders at the base of the falls. Those depressions were formed over many years through the process of erosion, due to the force of water continuously pounding against the rock.

Rumor had it that you could tuck behind the falls and into those depressions, where you could actually stand bone dry. We didn't dare attempt that in the springtime, as the current was way too swift. But in the late summer and early fall, when the water flow had substantially slowed, it was fairly safe. At least that was the rumor.

That next fall when Brice and I were at the river and the conditions were right, we waded in below the falls, made our way around the boulders, and stumbled right into one of those little caves. Sure enough, we were able to stand inside and stay mostly dry. What's more, with the continuous flow of water over the front of the cave, and the darkness of the rock behind, we were completely hidden from view.

If not for the constant noise of the falls and the wet ground, that would have made for a great hideout. Of course, it wouldn't work for a long stay. There wasn't much room to sit, and you'd eventually get tired of standing.

In our exploration around the base of the falls, we discovered several pools of water between the boulders. Those pools would form as the water level receded with the lower flow in late summer and early fall.

Fish (primarily carp and catfish) would swim into those pools, and they'd get trapped when the water level dropped. You could reach into those pools and catch fish with your bare hands. So we did. Some of those fish were fairly big, but they were real slimy and hard to handle.

I later learned that this type of "fishing" is a thing. It's known as noodling, and it's great sport in a number of states. However, Idaho is not one of them; it's illegal there.

Well, we didn't know we were noodling, and even if we did, we didn't know it was illegal. And I have to believe it would only be illegal if we kept the fish. We never kept any fish; for us, it was strictly catch and release. Worst case, I suppose we could have been charged with harassing the fish.

I'd prefer to think that what we were doing was more like examining the fish. It was sort of a science project. Who knows? We could have won a blue ribbon for it. In any case, I am certain that the statute of limitations on whatever crime we may have committed *there* has long since expired.

On one occasion, Brice reached into one of those pools and felt something sharp. When he pulled his hand out, it was bleeding. He was convinced that he was bitten by a carp.

I don't think carp can bite, since their teeth are set way back in their throats. If anything, it could have been a catfish sting, but that would . . . well, *sting*. Brice didn't seem to be in enough pain for me to believe it was a catfish sting. I know because I've experienced one.

If you ask me, I think Brice cut his hand on a rock and wanted to blame it on something other than himself! Because that's exactly what I would have done.

Venturing just beyond the river, we discovered Porter Canal. It was the equivalent of a slow, lazy river. Other than one potential hazard, it appeared to be an ideal spot for tubing.

The potential hazard was a parking lot built for a local hotel over a section of the canal, about 300 feet in length. That effectively created a tunnel, with limited clearance between the surface of the water and the bottom side of the parking lot above.

Despite the potential hazard, that section of the canal looked to be easily navigable. Though we had never observed anyone else floating it, that wasn't about to slow us down. We were happy to start a new trend.

Brice and I rounded up some float tubes and returned to the canal a few days later. Summer was ending, and we were anxious to do a little tubing before school started in the fall. We put into the canal a few hundred yards upstream of the tunnel.

We had picked the perfect day. The sun was hot, and the water was refreshingly cool. As we approached the tunnel, we could see that there would be plenty of clearance for us to float right on through.

Inside the tunnel, we observed swallows flying to and from mud nests that they had built in the upper corners, where the canal walls met the bottom side of the parking lot. We were able to get fairly close as we floated along, just a few feet below them.

Negotiating the tunnel was as effortless as a Sunday stroll. But conditions in the tunnel were not ideal. It was a little dark as we drifted through the center section, and we couldn't see much other than the light emanating from either end of the tunnel. It was also somewhat hard to hear each other due to the echoing of our voices, the sound of water flowing, and the rumble of cars driving on the parking lot directly above.

We floated right on through, exiting the tunnel without incident. A few hundred yards downstream, we made our way to shore, and climbed up and out of the canal. We walked back up the road to do it again and made half a dozen or so runs before calling it a day. We couldn't wait to get back for some more tubing but never had a chance before school started back up and cold weather set in.

At the first opportunity that next spring, right after school ended for the year, we finally had a chance to head back to the canal. Brice and I told a few of our friends how much fun it was and convinced them to join us. We rounded up our tubes, and they all managed to corral some of their own. With tubes in hand, we headed for the canal.

We put in at our usual spot, a few hundred yards upstream of the tunnel. I noticed that the water was much colder than I remembered.

That was to be expected for the time of year, but I didn't give it much thought.

What I failed to notice was that the water level was significantly higher than it had been when we floated the canal the previous summer. That also should have been expected for the time of year, due to the high run-off from snow melt. Not noticing that difference in the water level was a near–fatal mistake.

As we approached the tunnel, it quickly became apparent that the higher water level was going to cause us some trouble. There would not be enough clearance for us to float through if we remained on our tubes. As soon as we reached the tunnel, we slid off of our tubes and swam alongside.

At the entrance, there was just enough room for our tubes to float freely. However, as we got farther in, our tubes began to wedge against the bottom of the parking lot. At about the halfway point, there was barely enough room for us to keep our heads above water.

At that point, we each had a decision to make: stay with your tube, which would serve as a life preserver, but it would be an impediment to making progress downstream, or leave your tube and trust your ability to swim out on our own.

It was hard to hear in the tunnel under normal circumstances, but with the increased water flow and more kids yelling, it was impossible. None of us could make out what anyone else was saying, so there was no coordinated decision on what to do. It ended up being a free-for-all: every kid for himself.

Independently, we each made the decision to stay with our tube. Dragging our tubes got harder and harder as we worked our way downstream. Toward the end of the tunnel, we were repeatedly having to go under water to get leverage enough to drag the tubes, moving them only about a foot with each pull, then coming back up for air.

After what seemed like an hour, but may have only been about five or ten minutes, we all made it out the other side, hanging onto our tubes and sucking for air. It was a miracle that no one drowned. We were all exhausted, scratched up, and shook up, but otherwise, no worse for the wear.

We never went tubing in that canal again. Though Brice and I somehow managed to stay out of harm's way in the river, the canal nearly got us. We could have easily drowned, or worse, we could have been grounded for life. Mom was proven right again: she was two for two with her rules that we absolutely should have followed.

CHAPTER 10

THE GAME (BROKEN WINDOWS)

I begin this chapter with another quote from my favorite humorist, Yogi Berra: "Baseball is ninety percent mental. The other half is physical."[10] What I love about many of Yogi's quotes is that they are both funny and wise at the same time. In this quote, the math doesn't quite add up. But when you play the game, it really does feel that way. Baseball may not be as active as some other sports like basketball, football, or soccer, but there *is* a lot of thinking to the game.

Baseball was a huge part of my youth. My childhood memoirs would not be complete without a considerable amount of discussion on the subject. I dedicate this chapter to baseball, America's game.

Dad played on a recreational softball team when I was growing up. He was a decent player, but for him, it was just as much about the social aspect as it was about the athleticism and competition. Dad was definitely competitive, and he liked the physical activity, but even more, I think he liked to party with the guys at the end of the game.

I would tag along with Dad from time to time to watch him play. I didn't understand a whole lot about the game, but I was intrigued by it. The more I saw of it, the more I liked it. Dad was thrilled when I began to show an interest.

With the Angels practically playing in our backyard, we had an opportunity to watch a lot of ball games. We could partially see the games from our dining room window. The perimeter fence blocked most of the outfield from our view, but we could pick up on whatever we were missing by listening to the play–by–play action on the radio. It wasn't the same as actually being there, inside the stadium, watching from the stands. But heck, it was free, and we could watch from our window any time we wanted.

One of our neighbors had built a shed at the back end of his property, as close as he could position it to the edge of the alleyway. He built the shed high, a little higher than the ballpark perimeter fence, and installed bench seats on the roof. From those seats, he could see just about the whole ballpark; the far end of right field was about the only part of the field obscured from his view. He had also run an electrical line from his house to the shed to provide power for a radio.

Most every night that the Angels were playing at home, this neighbor would sit atop his shed with friends and other neighbors to watch the game while listening to the radio broadcast. Well, it didn't take long for Dad to ingratiate himself with that neighbor. Soon thereafter, Dad was on the invitation list to watch games from the top of the neighbor's shed.

Dad let me tag along with him a few times when it wasn't a school night. I have to hand it to that neighbor. He took full advantage of the opportunity he had, living where he did. Watching a ball game from the top of my neighbor's shed was better than watching from our window, but it was still not as good as actually being there.

Then there was that. Dad would take me to the stadium on special occasions to actually be there, to watch the games, up close and personal. There's really nothing like it. At the stadium you can hear the snap of the ball hitting the glove, the crack of the bat connecting with the ball, and the roar of the crowd responding to the action on the field.

As we watched the Angels play, Dad would explain to me the intricacies of the game. When I was a little older, he took me to a major league baseball game to see the Angels play at Anaheim Stadium in California. That was during one of our family vacations to Disneyland. The rest of the family went to Knott's Berry Farm. I don't think any of them really cared about going to a major league game, and I didn't really care about going to another amusement park.

Going to that major league game at Anaheim Stadium was a special time between me and my dad. From watching Dad play, then attending all of those games with him, I learned a lot about baseball before I ever started playing, myself. I also learned a lot about Dad. He and I were building a close relationship through our mutual affection for the game.

Dad could see how much I was beginning to enjoy baseball, and he determined to get me into an organized league. But first, he would have to get me ready. Dad bought me a brand–new Rawlings leather glove and a Louisville Slugger bat. We already had plenty of balls, thanks to some of the better hitters who played in the Pioneer League at Angels ballpark.

Dad and I played a lot of catch in the backyard. He taught me the fundamentals of throwing: take the ball all the way over the top, aim for your target's chest, follow through with your arm and hand; catching: watch the ball all the way into your glove, use two hands whenever possible, get your body down and in front of grounders; and batting: get your feet squared away, keep the bat up off your shoulder, keep your eye on the ball, take a level swing. In Dad, I had my own personal trainer.

We didn't have batting cages with pitching machines when I was a kid, at least not in my neck of the woods, so Dad rigged up a baseball on a string that he would swing over his head to give me some batting practice. I don't know where he got the idea for it, but I thought it was ingenious. I always assumed it was Dad's invention because he had to tweak the design after the first few batting practices.

Dad originally used kite string, but that would break after one or two good contacts with the ball. He replaced the kite string with some black, nylon string, and that solved the problem. I don't believe we ever broke the nylon string.

Another reason I think the baseball on a string was Dad's invention is that any company that sold such a thing would likely be sued. It was almost a guarantee that, sooner or later, the person swinging the ball around was going to get hit. And there was a good chance that the person who got hit would get seriously hurt. It was just a matter of time.

At first, Dad didn't have to worry much about getting hit. When I did connect with the ball, I wasn't swinging all that hard, and Dad was usually able to avoid getting hit. But as my batting improved, Dad had a harder time getting out of the way. He got hit more and more frequently. After a few seasons, that ball on the string mysteriously disappeared.

Dad got me a pitch–back net that would return my throw so I could practice when he wasn't around. During one of my solo practice sessions, an overthrown ball ended up going through a large plate–glass window in the basement rental unit, coming to rest on the front room floor. Fortunately, nobody was living there at the time.

I panicked, not knowing what to do. That was a big window, and I didn't want to get in trouble for breaking it. I had no idea what the consequences might be, but whatever they were, I didn't want to face them. So rather than take responsibility for it, I came up with what I thought was a logical explanation for what happened; an explanation that would clear me of any wrongdoing.

I entered the rental unit and swapped the worn–out practice ball that had come to rest on the floor for a fairly new–looking home run ball that I had recently retrieved from the backyard. Then I rehearsed the story repeatedly in my mind, and nervously waited for Dad to get home from work at the end of the day.

As soon as Dad walked in the door, I approached him with my story. That was my first mistake (after the broken window, of course). I should have given him some time to get settled in, fix himself a martini, and relax a little. After consuming a little alcohol, he may not have been as astute to pick up on the flaws in my story.

I told Dad, "I noticed that the front window of the rental unit is broken. It must have been caused by a home–run ball from the Angels' game last night."

In that last sentence, I made my second and third mistakes. I was already at three strikes, and Dad knew it.

I didn't know that Dad knew it, so I continued, "I saw the ball lying on the floor inside the rental unit when I happened upon the broken window myself. It's still there if you want to see it."

Dad waited patiently for me to finish, then replied, "I don't need to see the ball, son, because I know that you're lying."

Apparently, Dad knew a few things that I didn't know. He knew that if a home run ball was to blame for the broken window, it would have been the longest home run ball ever hit from that park. That may have been possible, but it was not probable.

Dad also knew that a home run ball could not have been hit any-where near our house the night before because the Angels were out of town that week. So that was not even possible.

That was it. Three strikes and I was out.

Dad responded, "Now start over, and tell me how it really happened."

I broke down and confessed that I had accidently overthrown the ball and broken the window myself. I didn't get a whoopin' for breaking the window, but I did get one for lying about it.

By the spring after I turned nine, it was time for me to join a team and start playing ball. Dad found out when tryouts were being held for the Little League organization in our neighborhood, and he sprang into action. He spent some time hobnobbing with some of the coaches in the league. They gave him the lowdown on what they'd be looking for at the tryouts.

As the day of tryouts approached, Dad worked with me even harder, concentrating on some of my weaker skills to better prepare me. I spent a lot of time fielding grounders and having Dad throw hard and fast, right at me. That helped me to shake off any fear of getting hit with the ball. With that additional training, I was as ready as I could be.

Our Little League had three divisions: the Majors, the Minors, and the Affiliates. The Majors were for those kids with proven playing experience. The Minors were for those kids who showed promise but were not quite ready for the "big league." The Affiliates were for those kids who wanted to play, but didn't have much, if any experience.

It was expected that, with a little more experience, kids who played in the Affiliates would be able to work their way up to the Minors, and kids who played in the Minors would be able to work their way up to the Majors.

At tryouts, the coaches for the various teams in each division would watch the kids throw, catch, and bat. The coaches all had clipboards on which they would take notes as they sized up the prospective players. Following the tryouts, the coaches would get together to hold a draft of sorts. According to Dad, who was witness to some of those drafts in later years, they involved some fairly high–stake negotiations.

Finally, the day of tryouts arrived. The morning sky was overcast, the clouds carried a slight drizzle of rain, and my stomach was all in a knot. I had a lot of anxiety over making the Majors. I didn't know quite how to handle it. My anxiety was literally making me sick, but I had to get out there and perform. I had to make the Majors. As far as I was concerned (and Dad certainly did not put this on me), failure was not an option.

To ward off the morning chill, I started out wearing a sweatshirt over my T-shirt, and to stay dry, a rain jacket over the sweatshirt. Between my anxiety and the multiple layers of constrictive clothing, I was not very nimble or coordinated on the field. Needless to say, the tryouts started off a little rough for me. I missed some easy fly balls; I was misjudging them, slow getting to them, and outright dropping them.

About an hour into the tryouts, the rain quit, and it started to warm up. I ditched the rain jacket and sweatshirt, and my anxiety seemed to leave with them. I was able to settle down and focus on the basics. From that point on, I caught just about everything that came my way: pop flies, line drives, grounders . . . no problem. I also had some good "at-bats."

I was relieved when the tryouts ended a few hours later. I was just hoping that the coaches would be able to see past my initial jitters and focus on how well I played after that.

A few days after the tryouts, I learned that I had been selected for a team. I made the Majors. I was on cloud nine. I'd like to think that it was all a result of my impressive throwing, catching, and batting skills. That may have very well been true. But I wouldn't be surprised if my dad and a six-pack of beer had something to do with it.

The team that "drafted" me didn't have a cool, daunting name like many of today's youth sport teams, like the Destroyers, the Raptors, or the Scorpions. Those names alone can put the fear of God in a team's opponents. And when those teams with cool names know how to play, they are feared all the more.

I was drafted by the Red Hats. That name left a little to be desired. Fortunately, our opposing teams' names were no better: the Dark Blue Hats, the Light Blue Hats, and the Green Hats. I just don't see how a hat of any color could scratch up an ounce of fear in an opponent.

At least our opponents' hats didn't scare us any more than ours scared them. Any fear we were to instill in our opponents would have to be through our abilities to play the game, and those abilities alone. In spite of the lame name, I was happy to be on a team.

I had a great coach: Coach Jim. He knew baseball better than anyone else I knew, even better than my dad. Coach Jim worked with us on the fundamentals of the game and drilled us on the various scenarios we might encounter. Before the ball was even hit, we knew where to make the throw, who would receive the throw, and who would back up the throw.

**My Little League team, the Red Hats, with Coach Jim, 1968
(I'm the kid kneeling in the front, lower right)**

At bat, Coach Jim taught us to "run it out" every time we hit the ball, regardless of whether or not it was a pop-up or an otherwise apparent easy out. We would make our opponents execute. More often than not, they would execute well. But occasionally, they would make errors, just like everyone else. The difference was, we were coached to capitalize on their errors. It was amazing how often that bit of coaching paid off.

Coach Jim really cared about the players on his team. He taught us as much about character and sportsmanship as he did about the game. Each season, Coach Jim would take a rag-tag group of new recruits and meld them with the veteran players into a solid, cohesive team.

Coach Jim instilled in us a sense of concern for one another and pride in the team. In competition, it was okay for us to chatter a little when our opponents were at bat, but there was no room for trash talk or denigrating any player, ever.

Unfortunately, not all of the coaches in our league were like Coach Jim. One of the coaches recruited a midget and a dwarf to make it hard for our pitchers to hit the strike zone—not kidding. Those kids were not allowed to swing the bat, and they usually drew a walk. Sure, their on-base percentages were high, but they were just being used.

I felt bad for those kids. It was really just sad to watch. At the end of the day, I don't believe that was in those kids' best interests. And I don't think it helped build character and sportsmanship for the other kids on their team, either.

Under Coach Jim's management, the Red Hats were always the number one or number two team in the league. The Dark Blue Hats were our nemesis. When we were number one, they were number two and vice versa.

I suspect the Dark Blue Hats had a coach who was about as good as Coach Jim. I don't say that just based on their win/loss record, but on the similar way their coach treated his players.

After each win, Coach Jim would have us all pile into the bed of his pickup truck, and he would drive us down to the local A&W. He would treat us all to a frosty cold mug of root beer.

You'd be arrested for driving a bunch of kids around in the bed of a pickup truck today. And I know there is no nutritional value in a mug of root beer. But so what? That's what we did, and we loved it.

If we lost the game, well, better luck next time—no root beer for us.

On one occasion, after a particularly tough game against the Dark Blue Hats where we played our hearts out and lost, Dad took me to the A&W for a root beer. He wanted to reward me for a game that I played well, even though my team lost.

As I was enjoying that cold, refreshing soda, I noticed that the Dark Blue Hats were there, too, piled in the bed of their coach's pickup truck. They were there to celebrate their win with a frosty cold mug of root beer, just like our team did when we won. It made me think that there must have been times when some of their players observed our team celebrating in similar fashion.

While I was disappointed that we lost, I was happy that I had played well. And I had to hand it to the Dark Blue Hats. As a team, they all played well, and they came away the victors. They deserved to celebrate. Looking back on that now, I realize that was the kind of sportsmanship Coach Jim was teaching us.

I played for Coach Jim and the Red Hats for four years. I mostly played third base, though I learned and could play just about any position. I even spent some time as a relief pitcher when Coach was really desperate. In my last two years, I could hit an occasional "out of the park" home run, and I made the Snake River All Stars for our league those years. I was at the top of my game.

Then the bottom dropped out. My parents split up after my last year of Little League. My dad, the driving force behind my interest in baseball, went AWOL. I tried playing organized ball on a city league, but I had to start back on the bottom, as a not–so–big fish in a very big pond.

Mom struggled to get me to practices, which were on the other side of town. I mostly rode the bench that year. Without anyone to motivate me, encourage me, or cheer me on, I lost interest. That was the end of my baseball career.

CHAPTER 11

THE KID (BROKEN NORMS PART I)

A few years after I started playing Little League baseball, Brice was old enough for the tryouts. Unfortunately for Brice, Dad did not invest the time to work with him and prepare him for it like he had done for me. Dad and Mom's marriage was beginning to unravel, so Dad moved out. After that, he really wasn't around much to help out and to be there for us kids.

Brice was every bit as athletic as me, but without the training and practice that I had leading up to my tryouts, it was tougher going for him. Mom was the one who was there for Brice. She didn't know much about baseball, though. She wasn't one to play catch, and she was certainly not one to put herself in harm's way with twirling a ball around on a string for batting practice.

Though Mom was no substitute for Dad when it came to teaching and coaching, I give her credit for showing up and doing what she could. And she did manage to get Brice to the tryouts at the right place and time. As a result of those tryouts, Brice ended up on the Red Hats team in the Affiliates division.

I know Brice was disappointed with that. He would like to have been selected to play at a higher level. With a little coaching, he could have been. But like everything else in his life, Brice just seemed to take it in stride. At least we were in the same "franchise," for whatever that was worth.

Brice played in the Affiliates division for a short time before working his way up to the Minors, still within the Red Hats franchise. He was a stud in that division. Brice's coach was often referring him for a move up to the Majors. But every time Coach Jim went to watch one of their games (always looking for potential recruits), Brice would underperform.

Brice knew he was underperforming, but he couldn't understand why. I suspect he was experiencing some of the same anxiety I experienced at my tryouts a few years earlier. I was fortunate that I had enough time to recover and pull myself together while the coaches were still watching. Brice finished out his Little League career in the Minors, where he gave his team everything he had.

After we had gained some experience in Little League, Brice and I were ready to join the pickup games at the Highland Park baseball field. We knew a few of the kids who played there because they attended our grade school. Most, however, were from the other school in the neighborhood.

We didn't know any of the kids from the other grade school, but they were all friendly enough. When Brice and I showed up with gloves in hand, we were warmly welcomed and invited to play.

On the days that Brice and I planned to play, it was always the same routine. I would jump out of bed, slam down some cereal or toast, and wait for Brice to eat so we could get to the ball field. However, Brice really enjoyed eating, and he went about it slowly and methodically. Waiting and watching was excruciatingly painful. . . for me.

The process would start with Brice plunking a slice of bread in the toaster.

Unconsciously, I would start tapping my fingers on the table.

When the toast popped up, Brice would meticulously cover it with peanut butter, working carefully to ensure a uniform thickness over the entire surface.

More anxious finger tapping.

Atop the layer of peanut butter Brice would apply a generous dollop of honey, skillfully spreading it to ensure a consistent top coating.

Still more anxious finger tapping.

With the masterpiece complete, it was *bon appétit*! Brice would take a big bite, and chew, and chew, and chew, savoring every delicious morsel, all the while breathing heavily through his nose.

More anxious tapping.

Brice would slowly take another bite, and chew, and chew, and chew, and deep nasal breathing.

Tap, tap, tap.

Repeat, repeat, repeat.

While Brice was chomping at his toast, I was chomping at the bit, anxious to get going. After what seemed to me like an eternity, the slice of peanut butter and honey toast was wholly consumed.

Finally, I would think. *Now we can go.*

But wait! Brice wasn't finished. In fact, he was just getting started. He would usually go for a second, and occasionally, a third round.

"Arghhhh!" *Tap, tap, tap, tap, tap, tap . . .*

If God was teaching me patience, I was a slow learner, because that routine was repeated day after day after day. When Brice was finished with breakfast, he could move. We'd get to the park as fast as we could, but more often than not, the game would have already started (thanks a lot, Brice!). Fortunately, the other players were gracious and would find a way to work us in.

On most fair–weather summer days, the baseball games would come together quite organically. There was not much organization or structure to them. There were, however, a handful of kids who seemed to be in charge. They would make all of the decisions, like choosing players for each team, choosing which team batted first, etc.

These kids weren't necessarily the oldest. Rather, they were the kids who showed up to play on a regular basis and were most familiar with the rules of the game. These were the "core" players. All the other kids would show up more sporadically and/or they just hadn't played much. They were content to play when they could, and they would take orders from the core players.

By the end of that first summer, Brice and I knew most of the kids fairly well. As newbies, we weren't part of that inner circle of core players, even though we showed up regularly and knew the game pretty well. We would have to prove ourselves first. That didn't matter much to us; we were just happy to play.

When our neighborhood pickup games began that next summer, Brice and I found ourselves in the inner circle. I guess that meant we had officially proven ourselves. There was no formality to it, no selection committee, no voting. It was more of an unspoken recognition among the other core players.

As part of the inner circle, we had some pull among the other players. We got to help choose teams and make other important decisions. On those rare occasions when there were too many players, we got to help decide who would start and who would have to sit on the bench and wait for an opening. It was more common for us to not have enough players, so we had to help recruit more.

On more than one occasion, we had to go knocking on doors in the neighborhood in an effort to find more willing and able bodies. We would take just about anyone who could at least spell baseball. I didn't care too much for that aspect of the job, but I liked being recognized as a leader.

On any given day, there were probably more kids there of diverse racial, religious, and ethnic backgrounds than was representative of the community. Regardless of those differences, everyone was treated the same. We were all just ball players.

We would soon learn, however, that we were not immune to discrimination. But it wasn't based on race, religion, or ethnicity.

It's time for you to meet those neighbor kids, the ones who had such an impact on my life. I'll start with the first one I met. For now, I'll just refer to him as "the kid." If I could describe "the kid" in one word, it would be persistent.

No inventor in American history better personified the quality of persistence than Thomas Edison. When asked about his failure to find a longer-lasting filament for the light bulb, Edison replied, "I have not failed 700 times. I've succeeded in proving 700 ways how not to build a light bulb."[11] He was also quoted as saying "Our greatest weakness lies in giving up. The most certain way to succeed is to always try just one more time."[12]

"The kid" must have taken a page out of Edison's play book, because he was one of the most persistent individuals I've ever known. And from my observation, his persistence usually paid off. It opened doors for him, and it opened doors for others who benefitted from his persistence. I now introduce to you "the kid."

One morning, a few weeks after our games had picked back up for the summer, the day started in normal fashion. The sun was up, slowly warming the air through a cloudless azure sky. The tall, majestic pine trees were gently swaying in the soft breeze. The sounds of summer filled the crisp morning air, with birds singing their dawn chorus from the treetops, and cool, clear water rippling along the creek bed in the distance.

It looked to be just another day in paradise. (It seemed like paradise to us, anyway.) But it wasn't just another day. This day would be different. We could not have known it, nor could we have seen it coming, but this day would literally be a game-changer.

We gathered together, sized up the kids who were there, selected teams, and started to play. After a few innings, I noticed a kid watching from behind the backstop. With one hand he was gripping the chain link fence that protected him from overthrows and foul tips. With the other he held a baseball glove.

I'd seen this kid before, hanging around the park, always by himself. I didn't know who he was, and never paid him much attention. However, on this day, I couldn't help but pay attention. He just stood there, watching intently, silently, for nearly an hour.

I thought the kid was a little odd, just standing there. None of the other kids seemed to notice or give a care, but I couldn't let it go. If this kid wanted to play, why wouldn't he just say so?

Just as that thought was going through my mind, the kid hollered out to us, "Can I play?"

We had room for another player or two, so I didn't see any problem with it. I was thinking, *Of course he can play.* However, before I had a chance to respond, several of the other players responded loudly and firmly, "No!"

No one else said anything, one way or another. They just wanted to ignore the kid and get on with the game.

I was surprised. We had never before turned anyone down when there was room for more players.

The kid asked, "Why not?"

One of the older players responded, "Because you're a Dutton."

Ahhhh! Now I understood why no one wanted to let him play. That warning my siblings and I had been given when we first toured the neighborhood came back to me and was replaying in my mind: "Whatever you do, do not play with the Duttons!"

Bringing me back to the present, the kid responded, "I'm not a Dutton, I'm a Johnson."

That was met with several moments of silence. None of us knew exactly what to do or say next. Eventually, the older player who was doing most of the talking asked, "Then why do you hang around with the Duttons if you're not a Dutton yourself?"

The kid replied, "Because the Duttons are my cousins. But I'm not a Dutton. I'm a Johnson."

A few of the core players were not convinced. That called for a meeting at the pitcher's mound. (Because that's where baseball players meet when they need to talk things over). Brice and I were in favor of letting the kid play, and a few other players were on our side. Several players were opposed. They couldn't explain why they were opposed, other than the fact that they didn't believe him. They really thought this kid was a Dutton.

I argued, "He looks normal, and he seems like a nice kid, so he couldn't be a Dutton." (I had no idea what I was talking about. I'd never met a Dutton before, so how would I know anything about them? It just seemed like letting this kid play was the right thing to do). I may have been channeling my inner Monty Python using some *Holy Grail* witch logic, but after a little back and forth, my view held sway.

I hollered back, "If you're really a Johnson and not a Dutton, you can play."

Once again, the kid affirmed, "I'm a Johnson. My name is Eddie Johnson."

So with some trepidation among several of the other players, the kid—Eddie Johnson—was allowed to play.

I've never seen anyone move so fast to take a position on the field as Eddie did that day. You had to appreciate his exuberance. On a micro level, the change that occurred that day was easy to see if you knew where to look. The beaming smile on Eddie's face when he stepped up to the plate to bat gave it all away.

You could argue that that change was not such a big deal; after all, it was just one kid. But it was a big deal to that one kid; in that moment, it was the whole world to Eddie Johnson.

We could not have known how that change would impact things on a macro level. We had no high-minded motives. We had no fore-thought as to how it all might play out. We simply allowed Eddie to play, and in doing so, we unknowingly opened the door to something bigger. Something much bigger. It was coming, and it would affect the whole community in a very positive way.

Eddie was a few years younger than me, closer to Brice's age. He was a skinny kid, a little shorter than most of us, but probably average for his age. He came across as easygoing and laid back, but you could tell he was always thinking.

Eddie knew what he wanted, and he wasn't afraid to go after it. He could talk his way into just about anywhere he wanted to go and talk his way out of just about any trouble. You couldn't help but like the kid.

All things considered, Eddie was a solid player. In watching him play, it was clear that he was a student of the game. He knew the fun-damentals. He knew how to play, and he knew how to hustle.

Eddie had a raw talent for baseball. He wasn't the fastest kid out there, but he could read where the ball was going as it came off the bat and get there quicker than many of the well-coached players.

Eddie Johnson
(from 1973/74 junior high yearbook)

It was also clear that Eddie had not had much, if any, real coaching. He had a few bad habits that were typical of an uncoached kid, like making one–handed catches, swinging for the fence each time at bat, and going for extra bases when he shouldn't. A little coaching could help to shape this kid, this diamond in the rough, into a fairly decent ball player.

It was clear to me that Eddie was willing and able to learn. He just needed a chance. And then it came.

Somehow, Eddie caught the attention of Coach Jim. I wish I could say I helped to make that happen, but I can claim no credit for it. If I had to guess, I would credit Eddie himself.

Eddie likely asked Coach Jim directly if he could join the team. And knowing Eddie's persistence, he probably asked more than once. That approach had worked for him before, and not surprisingly, it worked for him again. Coach Jim promised Eddie that he'd see what he could do.

The date of the team tryouts for our league had already come and gone, so Coach Jim had to get the consent of the other coaches in the league to bring on another player. They okayed it. So with that, Eddie had his chance.

Eddie met up with Coach Jim at our baseball field after a pre-season practice, where he received an individual tryout. Eddie was up to the task, and he passed with flying colors. Coach Jim congratulated Eddie for his performance and welcomed him to the team.

Eddie had made it to the Majors completely on his own merits. He was a bona fide member of the fearsome Red Hats. The one stipulation Coach Jim gave Eddie was that he keep his nose clean.

Coach Jim was not referring to Eddie staying out of trouble with the law; that was not an issue. Coach Jim literally meant that Eddie needed to keep his nose clean. Eddie probably had hay fever or some type of chronic sinus infection because his nose was always goopy and dripping. Coach Jim kept an ample supply of tissues on hand specifically for Eddie's use.

Eddie really tried to keep his end of the bargain, but it had been going on for so long that it was a hard habit to break. It was tough for him to change his ways. Coach Jim knew that, and he showed Eddie a lot of grace with it. That was just another example of Coach Jim pouring into the lives of kids in the neighborhood.

One summer evening after Eddie had joined the Red Hats, Coach Jim took our team to an Idaho Falls Angels baseball game. I knew my way around the stadium, having been to a number of games before. I thought it would be a new experience for Eddie, though, as I didn't think his family could afford the tickets. I was prepared to take Eddie under my wing and show him around the stadium, but he seemed to know his way around better than I.

Eddie knew the layout of the stadium. He knew where the bathrooms were located, as if that mattered (read on). He knew where and what concessions were sold, and how much the various concessions cost. He also seemed to know several of the home team players by name. He had even collected a few of their autographs (not that any of them were famous then or later).

It was clear that Eddie had been to a fair number of games at Angels ballpark before. But how was that possible if his family didn't have much money?

I had underestimated Eddie. Whether he had come up with the money on his own for the tickets, or he had somehow managed to sneak his way in, I don't know. Whatever the case, it further proved his persistence. Eddie wanted to get in, and he found a way to do it.

That evening at the stadium was a real scorcher. It had been a hot, sweltering day, and the concrete floor retained much of that day's solar heat. Even after the sun had set, it brought little relief.

On the advice of Coach Jim, we had all been drinking plenty of water to stay hydrated. Eddie, who was sitting next to me, suddenly excused himself and left the stands. I watched him quickly make his way down the stairs and over to a grassy area at ground level just beyond the Angels' dugout on the first base side of the field.

That may have served as a beer garden of sorts. From my observation, it just looked like a place where fans would go to walk around and stretch their legs.

With people milling all around him, Eddie dropped to his knees, then lay face down on the ground. In that prone position, he lay there motionless for a minute or so. At first, I thought he was playing a joke on someone; you never knew with Eddie.

When I didn't see anyone in the vicinity paying Eddie much attention, I began to grow concerned, wondering what might have happened. Eddie eventually started to wiggle around, so I knew he hadn't passed out, but then I wondered if he might be having some sort of seizure.

Just as I was preparing to head down to check on him, Eddie stood up, walked back up the stairs, and sat down in his seat next to me. He continued to watch the game, as if nothing had happened. I asked Eddie if he was okay, and he replied "Yeah, all that water went right through me, and I really had to pee."

I wondered why Eddie didn't use the public restroom. It wasn't that far from where we were sitting. But in fairness to Eddie, there could have been a line of men waiting to use the restroom, and he probably knew that. I guess it was just as easy, and perhaps faster for him to walk down there and pee on the grass.

Though it was not something I would have done myself, I had to admire Eddie for his resourcefulness. He pulled it off without thinking twice about it, and for the most part, nobody was the worse for it. The fans down there had no idea they were standing in or walking through a puddle of pee.

I tried to mark in my mind the exact spot on the grass where Eddie had peed so I could avoid it in the future. Then I wondered how many other "spots" like that might be out there. Chances are, I had already stepped in one of those spots at one time or another. It would be impossible to avoid them all.

I concluded that it wouldn't be the worst thing in the world if I had stepped in it, but anything more would be disgusting. There's no chance I'd be rolling around the ground in that part of the ballpark.

CHAPTER 12

THE DUTTONS
(BROKEN NORMS PART II)

Now let's get to the other neighbor kids who had a such an impact on my life; the Duttons. These were the very kids I was advised to avoid. Will Rogers, another great American humorist said, "Good judgment comes from experience, and a lot of that comes from bad judgment."[13]

Will was right. It was bad judgment on my part to blindly follow the advice of others, but it was a good experience in that I learned from it. In this chapter, I'll share the journey of how I worked through that, and what I learned from it, how that experience taught me something about developing good judgment and building true friendship. I'd like to introduce you to my neighbors, my friends: the Duttons.

Not long after Eddie started playing ball with us, he took Brice and me aside and asked, "Hey, would it be okay if my cousins play? They're Duttons."

The way Eddie asked the question, it was clear that he knew that would be a problem. I was thinking, *What have we done? We let Eddie play, and now this?* I didn't answer right away.

Eddie continued, "They're good ball players, every bit as good as me. They're good kids, and they just want a chance to play."

Eddie must have sensed that his best chance of getting his cousins into the neighborhood pickup games was through Brice and me. Maybe that's because we were the new kids on the block, and he figured we would not be so hard over against them. Or maybe he saw something in us that we didn't see ourselves, just a hint of caring and compassion. Whatever the case, we didn't bite.

We told Eddie, "We'll give it some thought." But we didn't really give it much thought. We brushed it off and tried to forget about it. It was one thing for us to let Eddie play; it would be quite another to let the Duttons play.

The next time we saw Eddie, he asked again, "What do you think about letting my cousins play?"

And again we told him, "We'll give it some thought." And again we didn't give it much thought.

As mentioned before, Eddie was nothing if not persistent. He continued to pursue, and we continued to evade. We liked Eddie, but he was putting us in a tough spot.

On one hand, we had been convinced that we shouldn't let the Duttons play. There was no ambiguity in the warning we were given by our tour guide in that early tour of the neighborhood: "Whatever you do, do not play with the Duttons!" On the other hand, it was hard to tell Eddie, "No!"

There was a sincerity in Eddie's voice when he spoke about his cousins. Brice and I were in a quandary. Could the Duttons really be all that bad? We couldn't continue to avoid the question. Either way, we'd have to make a decision.

We might have been young and stupid, but we weren't young and stupid enough to think that we had the answers to all of life's tough questions, so we went to the one person we knew who could offer some sound advice in social matters. We went to Mom.

In our brief description of the problem, we told Mom about Eddie, and explained how he had been asking us to let his cousins play. We emphasized the fact that his cousins were Duttons.

Mom looked a little dumbfounded, as if she had no clue as to who the Duttons were and why we couldn't let them play. Well, that's because she really didn't know who the Duttons were and why we couldn't let them play. She wasn't there for our tour of the neighborhood when we had been so enlightened. I had to spell it out for her.

I explained, "Eddie's cousins are Duttons, and we're not supposed to play with the Duttons!"

"Why not?" asked Mom.

I didn't have any better answer than what I was given when I asked that same question years before. I was stuttering and stammering, trying to come up with some other reason to support my case.

Mom interrupted, "It sounds to me like none of you even know the Duttons. You don't have a good reason to not let them play. You're treating them unfairly based solely on the talk of others. You need to give them a chance."

In no uncertain terms, Mom made it clear that we should tell Eddie his cousins could play. Then it was our turn to look dumbfounded as our jaws hit the ground. We had an answer, but it wasn't the answer we were expecting. We were expecting Mom to help us come up with an excuse to get Eddie off our backs and stop bugging us about his cousins. I had to make one more attempt at an easy out.

I replied "But Mom, they're Duttons."

Mom's response was clear and direct "And you're Murris. So what? The Duttons are probably not much different from you. You need to let them play."

The answer we got from Mom, which was really more of a directive, was contrary to the law of the land. Okay, maybe it was just a kids' law in a kids' land, but those were the laws by which we lived among our peers.

Our lives had suddenly become very complicated. We would either have to disregard Mom's advice, as if that discussion never happened, or we would have to agree to let the Duttons play and convince our peers to do the same.

Brice and I mulled it over for a few days, thinking through the possible consequences of whatever action we might take. We had a pretty good idea of the consequences for disregarding Mom's advice, if she was to find out. That was not a very big if. Mom always seemed to find out.

At a minimum, our consequences would be a pretty good tongue lashing, followed by some level of grounding. And there was a good chance that, after dealing with those consequences, we'd still have to do as Mom advised us in the first place.

Mom was right; none of us really knew the Duttons. That could be for better or worse. We had to hope for the better but be prepared for the worse.

We went back to the question I asked years earlier in our first tour of the neighborhood, "Why should we not play with the Duttons?"

Here are the only possible answers we could come up with, along with our line of reasoning in response:

1. "Maybe they're mean, and they'd want to hurt us."
   a) "It's not likely that they're mean. Eddie said that they're good kids. Eddie's a good kid, himself, and he's believable. He can be trusted."
   b) "If they're <u>a little</u> mean, we could just ask them to leave at any time. As a group, we have strength in numbers, so we wouldn't be in too much danger of being hurt."

c) "If they're <u>really</u> mean, they'd probably be locked up in jail or prison and we wouldn't be having this discussion."

2. "Maybe they are really sick, and they could make us sick."

a) "It's not likely that they're really sick. If they were really sick, we would likely be able to tell. And if we did catch something from them, our mom could just take us to the doctor's office, and they'd give us shots or something to make us better. So we wouldn't be in too much danger of getting sick."

We concluded that there really wasn't a good answer to that question. We had no rational basis to fear for our safety or well-being, but we still had some thinking to do. What might happen if we tried to convince the other players to let the Duttons play?

Here are the possible outcomes, as best we could imagine, along with our line of reasoning in response:

1. "They could flat out refuse and group us with the Duttons, just like they did Eddie because he hung around with them. If that happened, Brice and I, and maybe the whole Murri family, would be forever shunned. If the Duttons were being shunned for no good reason, the Murris could be shunned for no good reason, too."

a) "This was possible, and it would be an acceptable outcome. We'd be in the same camp as the Duttons, and we'd probably be in good company. Maybe they'd be our new best friends (you know, birds of a feather flocking together.)"

2. "A few of the players could refuse to play with the Duttons, and just walk away, never to play ball with us again."

a) "This was possible, and it would be an acceptable outcome. With them never playing again, it would be hard to round up enough players to field two teams. Worst case, that would end our neighborhood pickup games, and we'd just have to move on to something else."

3. "They could accept our request, and the Duttons could play."
    a) "This was possible, and it would be an acceptable outcome. Clearly, this would be the best–case scenario."

The bottom line was that all of these outcomes seemed quite possible. Worst case, our family is forever shunned by the community; best case, everyone walks away happy. In the end, we decided to take a risk, do the right thing, and hope for the best (avoiding Mom's wrath in the process).

We agreed to tell Eddie that the Duttons could play, and we'd lobby the other kids to go along with it. We needed to give the Duttons a chance, just as we did with Eddie.

The next time we saw Eddie, he approached us once again, and he started to ask, "What do you think about letting my cous—"

Before Eddie could even finish asking, I interrupted, "We decided that we want to let your cousins play."

Eddie was almost as excited to hear that as he was when we told him that he could play. Eddie was happy with that decision. We were happy with that decision.

It felt good to get that weight off our shoulders. We no longer had to evade the question or come up with lame excuses for why the Duttons couldn't play. It wasn't a done deal, though; not yet. We still had the burden of getting a majority of the other players to agree.

Before the start of our next game, we gathered everyone together at the pitcher's mound for a short meeting. We had asked Eddie to be there because he knew the Duttons. He could help to dispel any rumors or fears that the other kids might have. Eddie said he'd be there, but he was apparently running a little late.

While we waited for Eddie, I let the other kids know that we wanted their approval for something, but I wanted Eddie there for the discussion. I was still gathering my thoughts when he arrived.

Even with Eddie there, I wasn't sure how to start the discussion. While everyone was waiting impatiently to find out what the meeting was all about, I was trying to figure out how to best say it.

I started out, "I, ahhhh, we, well, the reason, ahhhh. After some ahhhh, well . . ."

As I struggled to put together a string of coherent words, the natives were growing restless. They wanted me to get to the point so they could play ball.

After a few minutes of being completely flustered, I ended up just blurting it out, "We're thinking about letting the Duttons play."

There was a long, uneasy silence as the other kids looked at me, looked at Brice, looked at Eddie, looked around at each other, looked down at the ground, then looked back at me. I don't know what was going through their minds; maybe they were trying to think through all of the bad things that could happen if we let the Duttons play, just as Brice and I had done. The difference is that these kids didn't have the luxury of time to mull it over. We needed an answer, then and there.

One of the older core players finally broke the silence. He replied simply, "Okay."

The others all shrugged, indicating they had no objection. Nobody asked any questions; nobody raised any concerns; nobody threatened to leave. Nobody even seemed to give it a second thought.

That was almost too easy. I was expecting at least some token level of resistance. After all, hadn't each of these kids played a role in keeping the Duttons away? If it was so easy to end the discrimination, why did it take so long to make happen?

Perhaps it was due to divine intervention; a few of the core players who had been so opposed to letting Eddie play, and would have been just as opposed to letting the Duttons play, didn't show up that day.

Perhaps it was because those who *were* there and may have been opposed were afraid to speak up.

Perhaps it was because we had already let Eddie play, and everyone could see that he was a normal kid, just like them. Why would his cousins be any different? Or perhaps it was because they just wanted to get on with the game and didn't want to spend any time arguing about it.

Whatever the case, it was decided. The Duttons could play!

The Dutton boys didn't come out and join us right away. I suppose there was some mistrust on their part. After being shunned by kids in the neighborhood for so many years, how could they be sure that things would be different? How could they be sure that they would be welcome and treated kindly?

I could envision Eddie talking it over with them and advocating on our behalf. He needed to convince them that we really did want to have them come out and play ball. Eddie must have worn them down like he did us because, after a few short weeks, the Duttons agreed to come out and give it a try. There again, I believe Eddie's persistence paid off.

We had no idea how many to expect, but when the Dutton boys finally did show up, there were only two. I remember thinking, *All of that fuss over two kids?* They approached us slowly and cautiously. We all gathered around while Eddie introduced them.

Joe, the oldest of the clan, was two or three years older than me; Terry was about my age. If there were other Dutton kids, I was not aware of it. We each introduced ourselves by name, and with the greeting, shook hands with Joe and Terry.

And that was that. Having dispensed with the formalities, there was no need to waste any more time. We divided into two teams, with Eddie, Joe and Terry in the mix, and the "home" team took the field. It was time to "Play ball!"

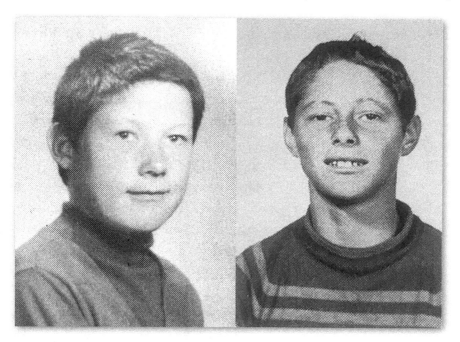

Joe Dutton, left (from 1968/69 junior high yearbook)
Terry Dutton, right (from 1970/71 junior high yearbook)

There it was: a simple act that had a profound impact on *one* family in the community. That simple act instantly ended any and all discrimination against the Duttons, at least within my little sphere of influence.

From that day forward, Joe and Terry were welcomed every time they showed up to play, whether Brice and I were there or not. They had been accepted by the other players. That simple act had a big impact on just about everyone in the community. The discrimination may not have ended everywhere and with everyone as instantly as it did with us, but I believe that marked the beginning of the end.

I never heard a word from the Duttons or any of the other players about what had transpired before that day. What was past was past. Everyone was happy to move on. I have to credit Eddie for opening the door, not only for himself, but for his cousins, as well. And he was right. The Duttons *could* play.

In the matter of baseball, Joe and Terry could throw, catch, and hit. They were not students of the game like Eddie, but they were good athletes, and they knew the basics. It was nice to have a few additional players for our neighborhood pickup games, too. These kids were ready, willing, and able to play, and they fit right in.

Joe was an average–size kid in both height and weight. As the oldest, he was the most responsible of the Dutton boys. He looked out for Terry. Joe may have been asked to do so by his parents. Whether or not that was the case, it seemed to come naturally for him. I don't recall ever seeing Terry without Joe, whether at our games or anywhere else in the neighborhood.

Joe had a calm, quiet, easy way about him. He was also somewhat cautious, and slow to build friendships. Whenever he looked at someone, it was as if he was sizing them up. More than anything else, Joe had a big heart. Once we got to know him, it was obvious that he really cared about us and the other kids.

Neither I nor any of my siblings ever heard Joe speak an unkind word about anyone. As I reflect back on that, I'm amazed that he could have had such a positive attitude, even toward those who had been so unkind to him and his family.

Terry was an average–sized kid in height, but sort of skinny. Where Joe was calm and quiet, Terry could be wiry and a little loud. He was not afraid to speak his mind. Terry had a good heart, and he found humor in just about everything. He could really make us laugh.

Terry also had a bit of a short temper and some social adjustment issues. It's hard to say whether those issues were the cause or effect of how he and his family had been treated. In any event, I think that's why Joe was so protective of him.

Joe had a gentle way of calming Terry down and helping to defuse his anger. As long as Terry was happy, everyone was happy.

I came to realize that the Duttons were not much different from us. Mom was right all along. They had a family who loved and cared about them, just like us. They loved God and country, just like us. They had feelings; they would laugh and cry just like us, be happy and sad just like us.

In some ways, however, the Duttons *were* different from us; they were different from us in ways that really didn't matter. The Dutton family was not as well off as ours financially. In comparison to our family, they were poor. I'm sure they made the most of what they had, but I suspect they didn't have many of the same opportunities we had.

The Duttons' house was somewhat smaller than ours. From all appearances, they had no front door. If there was a front door, I never saw it; it would have to have been always open. Whenever I walked by, I could see into the house. It was always the same; lots of people inside. I don't know what that was like for them.

We had six people living in our house, and I thought *we* were cramped. Our "cramped" living quarters was probably nothing like the Duttons'. We always had plenty to eat and nice clothes to wear. Even our hand-me-downs were in decent shape. Again, I don't know what it was like for the Duttons, but I have to believe life was harder for them.

Our parents were able to put us kids in organized sports (e.g., baseball and football), swim lessons, dance lessons, arts and crafts classes, and music lessons. We complained about some of those "opportunities," but at least we had opportunities. Whether or not we enjoyed them or took advantage of them was up to us.

I suspect the Duttons couldn't afford a lot of those opportunities for their kids. In spite of what they may or may not have had, the Dutton boys always had a positive attitude.

As Brice and I got to know Joe, Terry, and Eddie, we welcomed them more and more into our lives. It became more than just meeting up with them on the baseball field. They introduced us to various aspects of the neighborhood that were new to us, and we included them in some activities that were new to them, like our retaining wall–jump challenge.

Eventually, our whole family got to know and trust Joe, Terry, and Eddie. In just a few short years, Brice and I had developed a close relationship with them. They were more than neighbor kids who we allowed into our lives, and they were more than acquaintances. They were more like true friends. That was a long way from where we started.

Mom, who had been right about the Duttons from the start, allowed Brenda to join in our neighborhood games of night tag, knowing that they would help watch out for her. Brenda was only six or seven at the time. She wasn't able to keep up with us on her own two feet, so Joe and I would each grab an arm and swing her along with us as we ran.

Brenda wasn't the only girl in those night tag games. We were occasionally joined by a long–legged girl who lived between us and the Duttons. She was a year or two younger than me. I thought I was pretty fast, but that girl could smoke me. I attribute her speed to those long legs. Once again, I was humbled by the abilities of a girl, but I guess I was starting to get used to it.

I never got around to asking Joe or Terry or Eddie about all the crazy stuff that other kids said they did, like pooping in the pine trees at Highland Park. For one thing, I don't know how they could have possibly had time to go everywhere and do everything for which they were blamed. For another, I don't believe it was in their character to do so.

Even if they did half the things for which they were blamed, it wouldn't really matter to me. As long as no one got seriously hurt or killed, what difference would it make? Not to mention the fact that I did plenty of crazy stuff myself.

For all I know, the Duttons could have been blamed for some of the things *I* did. I suspect the Duttons were blamed for just about everything bad that happened in that neighborhood. Thankfully, that was changing.

CHAPTER 13

THE OTHER GAME

I met my neighbors, the Duttons, through the game of baseball. But I really got to know them through another game: the game of football. Where baseball is ninety percent mental and fifty percent physical (a previously quoted Yogi-ism), football is the other way around.

Without question, football is a more physical game. And it's not just the rough–and–tumble aspects of the game. In football, the players are generally in closer proximity to one another, much more so than in baseball.

In football, there are huddles, where team members often have their arms on or even around each other's shoulders; close formations, where players line up side by side on either side of the ball, where they come face to face with players from the opposing team; and tackles, where players from one team wrap their arms around the ball carrier from the opposing team, and where, more often than not, players from both teams end up in one big dog pile.

With all of that close, physical contact, the players can't help but get to know one another.

I fell in love with the game of football the first time I ever watched it played up close and personal. It immediately replaced baseball as my favorite sport.

The feelings I had toward the game at that time are captured in a quote by American pro football player, Odell Beckham, Jr.: "Football is my sanctuary. It's where I go to escape. It's where I'm most happy."[14] And taking it a step further, South Korean professional footballer Son Heung-min stated, "I want to play football until my body says, 'You can't run anymore: you're dead.'"[15] Though Son was referring to the game we in the USA call soccer, I would have agreed with his sentiments as it relates to our game of football.

I dedicate this chapter to the "other" game, the game we call football.

As a kid, I didn't watch much television. I didn't have time for it. I was too busy playing and exploring. When I did watch, it was usually in the fall during football season. Dad loved to watch professional football, and I liked to watch it with him.

We would occasionally place a high–stakes bet (two bits) on the outcome of a game involving our favorite teams. Brice eventually took an interest in professional football as well, and he joined in watching and wagering on the games.

Though betting on sports games was illegal at the time (as was any sort of gambling for a minor), I doubt that anyone in law enforcement would have cared a lick about our bets. It was all just for fun. Worst case for Brice and me if we lost, we may have had to forego a trip to Russ's Market to throw our money away on candy.

One year for Christmas, Mom and Dad gave us an electronic football board game, of sorts. It had a vibrating table on which we would set up our players. The player on offense would set up his team in some formation and hope that the ball carrier would move downfield for positive yardage, while the player on defense would set up a counter formation and hope his team would stop the ball carrier from making any forward progress.

When the players were ready with their formations, the table vibration would be turned on. The down would end when the ball carrier would either go out of bounds or come to a stop, at which time the table vibration would be turned off.

In principle, the game was good because it helped us to better learn the rules of football, but in practice it was highly frustrating. The vibrating table caused the players to move around somewhat spastically, and there was no telling what direction the ball carrier would go. There was not much opportunity for any kind of strategy.

Fortunately, the noise of the vibrating table was just as annoying to our parents as the game was to us, so they got us another, more quiet football board game: Samsonite Football.

Samsonite Football was played with cards, and it did involve strategy—strategy and luck. The "coach" of the team in possession would call out a play (rush, pass, or punt), draw a play card, and move the ball based on the outcome of that call as written on the play card. That game also helped us to better learn the rules of football, and it was not nearly as frustrating as the vibrating table game.

With Samsonite Football, each player is required to select a team name to write at the top of the score card. I always chose the Dallas Cowboys; Brice always chose the Washington Redskins. So Brice and I frequently played cowboys and Indians, but not in the traditional sense.

Brice and I could only sit around and play board games for so long. After a few years of that, we were ready for the real thing. We had watched enough football on television and played enough of the board games to know the fundamentals of this "other game."

We had plenty of experience running and tackling in our back-yard games of tag, but it wasn't the same. We wanted to play football, just like the professionals in the NFL, but we didn't have enough kids to put together two teams. None of our friends were really interested in football. They were more into baseball, basketball, and playing sandbox trucks.

We begged our parents to get us into an organized league where we could be part of a team, get a little coaching, and play football for real. We eventually wore them down, and they agreed to sign us up.

Me and Brice in our practice jerseys, 1969

In our community, the local organized football league was called Grid Kid Football. It was structured by grade rather than age. Since football is such a physical game, the league organizers wanted to compensate for variations in size within a grade. When I started playing, the league was allowing smaller kids to play down a grade if they were under certain weight limits.

I was one of those smaller kids. My parents had started Brett and me into elementary school early. I can understand why. Mom was dealing with four kids, ages five and under, when she enrolled Brett in first grade. The next year she followed suit with me, enrolling me in first grade at age five.

I was the youngest and one of the smallest boys in my class. Even so, I was able to hold my own against my peers, physically and academically. But Dad was not one to let an advantage go to waste. He exploited every opportunity that came his way, whether it would advantage him or someone else in the family.

So when I was in the seventh grade, Dad signed me up to play on the sixth–grade team. I just had to keep my weight below the prescribed upper limit to maintain my eligibility. I don't recall exactly what that limit was, but I believe it was somewhere around seventy-five pounds.

During the summer months, I was always burning more calories than I consumed, regardless of what and how much I ate. The weigh-in for football was in early fall, just after I started back to school. I was well below the limit for the sixth–grade team.

After football started up, Mom continued to weigh me in at home periodically. The scales soon indicated that I was gaining weight, and it didn't take long before I began to approach the limit.

My weight gain could be attributed to three factors: 1) I was in school all day, five days a week, and was a lot less active than I had been through the summer, 2) I was gaining muscle mass as part of my football training, and 3) I was growing in height. The scales were definitely tipped against me.

Mom cut me off from Hostess fruit pies, Twinkies, and all other "fattening" (but good-tasting) snacks. In their place I got grapes. Mom said I could eat as many as I wanted. That deal was a little too open ended (quite literally).

Not long after I was put on this special diet, I was feeling like I just couldn't satisfy my hunger. I longed for something more substantial, but I didn't want to risk being cut from the team for being overweight. So I stayed on plan.

One afternoon before practice, I consumed a generous portion of grapes. As Dad was driving me to practice, my stomach began to rumble. Initially, I ignored it, hoping it would just go away, but it didn't.

Shortly after practice started, I was in a bad way. I wandered off the field in search of a restroom or port-a-potty. Dad blocked my path and directed me back to the practice field. I tried explaining to him that I was feeling sick, but he wouldn't hear it. He thought I was just afraid of getting hit.

To this day, I don't understand how Dad could have been so wrong about me. I was not then nor have I ever been afraid of getting hit. I had never demonstrated any sort of timidity before in his presence or otherwise. I really *was* feeling sick.

Dad forced me to continue with practice . . . until I could no longer hold everything back. All of those grapes that went into my mouth exploded out the other end. Humiliated, I rushed off the field, and did an end-around Dad, who was trying to block my path again.

I dove into a dense patch of brush where I could clean up a little. When I emerged from the brush, I saw the expression on Dad's face go from anger to bewilderment to sorrow as he watched me slowly make my way toward him. I was physically and emotionally spent. I could not continue with practice, so we headed home.

The ride home was not pleasant, for obvious reasons. Dad explained that he forced me to continue with practice because he didn't believe I was sick. I guess that was his way of apologizing. As penance for his actions, he had to buy me a second pair of football pants that season.

Aside from having to keep my weight down, and the potential consequences of that, being able to play down a grade worked out well for me. It was a big confidence boost.

At the beginning of the season, I didn't know any of the kids on the team. They didn't give me much of a welcome, either. I was not in their class, which, from their perspective, may have had a double meaning. I brushed it off and focused on the game. I was just excited to be there, to be part of a team, and to play in an organized league.

I had a great coach who taught the fundamentals of the game, along with the detailed aspects of each position. As a defensive end, I learned the basics of blocking, tackling, and containing the play. We won a lot of games. I don't recall whether or not we won our division, but I do know that we won a lot more than we lost. I gave everything I had to help make that happen.

By the end of the season, I had earned my teammates' respect. I was on top of the world and looking forward to a long illustrious football career. That next season, the local Grid Kid Football league eliminated the option for smaller kids to play down a grade. My spirits were dashed. I would not be allowed to play for the coach and team I grew to love the previous season.

I signed up to play on my junior high team, but as the smallest player, I rode the bench the whole season. That put an end to my glory days of football. I completely lost interest and never played in an organized league again as a kid. On a positive note, I was no longer limited to grapes for an after–school snack. I was back to my favorite frozen Hostess fruit pies!

Shortly after Brice and I joined Grid Kid Football, we started playing in some neighborhood pickup games with Eddie, Joe, and Terry. Brice and I took what we learned in organized football and brought some of that "vast knowledge and experience" to our neighborhood games. We introduced some basic pass patterns and running techniques and threw in a few razzmatazz plays to boot.

Our neighborhood games were played in the Angels ball field. The Duttons considered that field their home turf. When it was not otherwise in use, they would make their way inside the ballpark, and play football in the outfield. Not too many kids in the neighborhood knew about that, so the Duttons could go there and play without being harassed. Eventually, Brice and I were accepted into *their* club, to play football in *their* park.

There were a few ways of getting into the park. The easiest and most direct approach for getting into the park was through an opening in the perimeter fence. During the Angels' off-season, a fence slat or two would occasionally come off. Most of us could skinny through the opening created by a single missing slat. How those slats came off, I have no idea. Really, no idea.

The fence would not normally be repaired until the start of the next season, so once we had a way in, we used it from late fall through early spring.

When there were no missing slats, we would have to resort to a different, and potentially more hazardous approach. That involved shinnying up the fence, climbing over, and dropping to the ground on the other side.

Teamwork was often required to help each other get up and over the fence. Dropping down was easy, but the landing would occasionally result in a twisted or sprained ankle. That tended to slow the injured party down, but it never resulted in anyone having to go back home (or to the hospital).

That's just how we played. Unless someone had an obvious broken bone, which would have required the bone to be protruding through the skin or some appendage to display in an unnatural position, the game went on.

It was a blessing to play football in the outfield of Angel ballpark. The grass field was level, and it was well maintained year-round. The city park fields were not nearly as nice.

During football season, Angels ballpark was used for Grid Kid Football games. The outfield would be marked for games with side-lines, yard lines, and goal lines. There were no uprights, but in all other respects, it was an "official" 100–yard football field. Playing on an official football field was an added bonus for our neighborhood pickup games.

I have to believe that the owners or managers of the ballpark were aware of us being there, but they never ran us out. I suppose since we weren't destructive—other than encouraging an occasional slat off the fence—they let us play.

We would agree to meet the Duttons to play at a prearranged time. Invariably, Brice and I would arrive late. We had to wait for him to finish breakfast. To his credit, I'd have to say that once his appetite was satisfied, Brice could hustle. His breakfast must have given him the energy he needed to sustain him at a maximum burn level all day.

After breakfast, we'd take off for the park on a dead run. As we'd make our way into the park, the guys would catch sight of us and lit-erally start jumping up and down with excitement.

As soon as they saw us coming, one of the kids would holler, "We get Blake!"

Another would respond, "Okay, we get Brice!"

Not only were we excited to be there, it was a rush to be wanted at that level, especially among these guys who we considered our peers. We felt like rock stars.

Baseball was a fair–weather sport for us, but we played football come rain, snow, sleet, or hail . . . well, maybe not hail.

We didn't need as many players for our football games as we did for baseball. Where we needed at least fourteen players for baseball (three infielders, three outfielders, and a pitcher on each team; the batting team could provide a catcher), we could get by with as few as five for football (one kid could play quarterback for both teams). With just Joe, Terry, Eddie, Brice, and me, we always had our five unless one of us was sick or too injured to play. When we had more than five, that was icing on the cake.

We played full–on tackle with no helmets, no pads. Sure, we'd get banged up a little, but we rarely had any serious injuries. It worked because we were all about the same size. On a few occasions, we had some much older kids join the game. That's when things could get rough, and we often would have more serious injuries.

The older kids were more developed, physically, and they could run right through us. I learned that the only chance I had of bringing them down was to grab their feet and hog tie them with my arms while being dragged downfield. I ended up getting kicked in the face on more than one occasion. I still enjoyed the game, but I enjoyed it more when the older kids weren't there.

There were two features of our neighborhood game that you could count on just about every time we got together to play. One involved Terry's football. The other involved Eddie's running style.

Terry owned the football. Brice and I didn't have one, nor did any of the other kids. I'm not sure why; a football couldn't have been that expensive. But it didn't really matter. Terry nearly always came to play, and when he came, he always brought his football. If he didn't come, there would be no game. No Terry, no football.

Terry was a solid player, but he was human like everyone else. When the game was going well for him, life was good. When the game was not going in his favor, Terry could get upset and threaten to leave.

Joe could usually calm Terry down completely on his own. Occasionally, though, we'd all have to do our part to apologize to Terry for whatever infraction we had committed. We didn't want him to go away mad, and we certainly didn't want him to go away with the football. On those few occasions when Terry did leave, Joe would leave with him, the football would leave with him, and our game would come to an abrupt end.

After a few years of playing, Terry's football was just about worn out. It was dry and cracking, and had lost most of its grip. About the time we were thinking we might need to get a football, ourselves, Terry showed up with a brand—new one.

I never met Terry's parents or grandparents or aunts or uncles or whoever might have come up with the idea of having him own the football, but I think they were pretty smart. If Terry didn't own the ball, we could have easily let him go away mad. As it was, we had to work it out with him so we could continue to play.

As for Eddie and his running style, I think it best to say that baseball was more his game. He was a hustler in both sports, and never left anything on the field. But in football, Eddie was not as good at reading the play while it was developing. Too many times when Eddie had the ball and was rushing for yardage, he would give up a lot of ground running in the opposite direction to evade a tackle. More often than not, he would be tackled for a huge loss.

On a rare occasion, Eddie would manage to evade tackles long enough to gain yardage. I suppose that's what kept him trying. But because Eddie failed much more often than he succeeded, we named that style of running after him.

Whenever someone, anyone, would run in the direction opposite the goal to evade a tackle, and get tackled for a big loss, we called it "pulling an Eddie." We used that phrase whether Eddie was around or not. Eddie may not appreciate that, but he really can't argue with it. It wasn't intended as a dig. That was just Eddie's signature play.

Brice and I not only loved the game, but over time, we grew to love Eddie Johnson and the Duttons. These were the kids we were told to avoid when we moved into the new neighborhood. These were the kids who had been wronged by the community for so many years.

Why they were not accepted is beyond me. By any measure, these were normal kids. These were the kids we eventually welcomed into our lives. These were the kids with whom we chose to play. These were some great kids, and I am proud to have called them my friends.

CHAPTER 14

LIFE LESSONS

I've learned a lot of lessons in my life. Most of what was important I learned during those formative years growing up near Angels ballpark in Idaho Falls.

I learned a lot of basic stuff, even after kindergarten. In grade school, I learned the basics of reading, writing, and arithmetic. As an added bonus, I learned some stuff that wasn't in my pocket dictionary. I guess most people learn that stuff from their parents at home. From my years in school, I learned that no subject was too hard if I really wanted to apply myself.

I learned a lot about adventure through exploring my neighborhood. I learned that it could be a lot of fun, but it could also be dangerous. Through some twisted logic, it seems that the more dangerous the adventure, the more fun it could be. I learned there's a fine line to walk between the two. That line is a little blurry when you're young and "invincible." Thankfully, it becomes a little more clear with age.

I learned a lot about sports from my dad and a few great coaches, like Coach Jim. I learned the basics of several individual and a few team sports. I learned how to fight, but more importantly, I learned when to fight, that it's only when there's something worth fighting for.

I learned a lot about discipline and practice. Whether it be individual or team sports, it didn't matter so much whether I won or lost as long as I did my best. In team sports, if I played well and my team won, the winning was icing on the cake.

I learned a lot about teamwork and sportsmanship. It wasn't all about me. It was about respecting my teammates and my opponents. It was about working together as a team to accomplish something greater than myself and building lasting friendships in the process.

In some ways, times have changed since my days of playing baseball for Coach Jim. When my kids' soccer team won a game, I couldn't pile them into the back of my pickup and take them to A&W for an icy cold mug of root beer. That would be neither nutritional, legal, nor safe. Rather, I would join the parents in celebrating every game, win or lose, by providing the kids with healthy, nutritious snacks.

In other ways, times really haven't changed that much. I was able to take a ragtag bunch of kids, teach them the fundamentals of the game, be there for them, and provide a few life lessons along the way.

I am forever indebted to my dad and Coach Jim for coaching me, being there for me, and teaching me some valuable life lessons along the way.

I learned a few positive character traits, too. I learned patience while waiting for Brice to finish breakfast. I learned humility in losing the spelling bee to a girl in my class. I learned obedience after breaking rules and nearly drowning in the canal. I learned honesty when I was caught (or is it cot?) in a lie after throwing a baseball through the window. And I learned kindness and compassion by welcoming some neighborhood kids into my life.

I've often asked my children to consider how they would like to be remembered, what they would like to have written on their tombstone. Perhaps a little morbid, but I think it helps us determine how we would like to live our lives. I can't think of much better praise than to have it said that I was patient, humble, obedient, honest, kind, and compassionate.

I'm thankful for the parents, teachers, and coaches who came alongside and helped to build character in me during my youth. Through their teaching, through their coaching, through the examples of how they lived their lives, they helped to make me who I am. They helped to build in me a solid foundation.

We know that the building doesn't end with the foundation. We continue to build on top of that foundation. I have not finished learning. I will always be a work in progress.

What I *have* learned, I am compelled to pass along to others, through parenting, teaching, and coaching. And perhaps in writing this book, I have been able to pass along to the reader some of what I have learned.

BROKEN RULES

By the grace of God, I survived my childhood. I went on to get married, have children, enjoy a long and illustrious career, and make my mark in this world.

I might not have survived if things had turned out differently with some of the poor choices I made, those times when I broke rules that were put in place for my safety. Like the times I chose to play around the busted wood piles and the old shack in the vacant lot next door. And like the times I jumped off the Johns Hole Bridge into the Snake River, went exploring under the falls, and went tubing in the Porter Canal.

I knew those activities were against the rules, but I did them anyway. I didn't have the experience or maturity to recognize the risks I was taking. It just seemed like a lot of fun . . . until it wasn't.

It wasn't fun getting a rusty nail from the wood pile stuck through my foot, having tetanus set in, going to the ER, and getting a shot to treat it. It was no fun getting my float tube wedged in the canal beneath the hotel parking lot, having to swim out while dragging my tube behind, and nearly drowning. I couldn't imagine how horrible it would have been if Brice had drowned. I should have been looking out for him. Instead, I led him headlong into danger.

Mom had laid down rules for our safety. They were meant to be followed, but in my infinite wisdom, I thought I knew better. I broke the rules. I paid a price for breaking some of those rules, but the price could have been much higher.

Looking past the foolish years of my childhood (plus a few crazy times as a young adult in high school and college, where alcohol was usually a contributing factor), I came to the understanding that rules were made for a reason. (Imagine that!) They were not only made for my benefit, but also for the benefit of others.

I was no longer the rebel of my youth. My change in attitude wasn't necessarily a conscious decision, and it certainly wasn't made overnight. It was more of a metamorphosis as I slowly matured and learned from my experiences. I became a rule follower.

I made my share of mistakes along the way. We all do. We all make choices in life. We can either choose to learn from the mistakes of others or we can choose to learn for ourselves.

Learning from the mistakes of others is clearly an easier, less risky, less painful way to go. Unless we want to make the same mistakes as those before us, we need to listen and take heed. In other words, we need to be obedient. We need to follow the rules.

Being obedient won't remove all risks in life, but it will keep us from making unforced errors. In soccer parlance, the term is "making own goals," and those are probably the biggest mistakes you can make. We need to avoid making own goals in life.

Based on my personal experiences growing up, I always felt that I would consider myself fortunate if my own kids pulled half the shenanigans I pulled and survived to see adulthood.

My wife and I laid down rules for our kids' safety. I shared some of my life lessons with them, but I was careful to avoid passing along the details of some of my more risky experiences. I didn't want to give them any excuses for making poor decisions of their own.

How could I argue with the retort, "I don't know why you're so upset, Dad. You did worse, and you managed to survive!"? My kids would have enough temptation without having the details of my childhood experiences to justify their behaviors.

As it turns out, I am very fortunate (actually, very blessed). All three of my kids made it safely through to adulthood, even my mini-me! I will probably never know all of the shenanigans they pulled, and I don't think I really want to know. The key point is: They made it. Thank God they made it!

Broken Windows

My parents lived at a time when a man's word was his bond. Deals were often made with the shake of a hand. Dishonest business-men were commonly run out of town. Cheaters were usually disgraced in their communities.

Honesty and integrity were esteemed as the greatest virtues. Mom and Dad worked hard to instill those virtues in us kids. It's no wonder they considered lying, the antithesis of honesty and integrity, to be the greatest sin. Lying was simply not tolerated, period.

I'm guessing that just about every kid in the country has had a broken window experience or something equivalent. And I suspect that most kids have had some of the same thoughts that I had going through my mind in the aftermath. Kudos to those who chose to be honest right from the start.

Unfortunately, I think those kids who choose honesty from the start are in the minority. The rest of us have, at one time or another, stretched the truth or made something up from whole cloth. We do everything we can to avoid taking responsibility for our actions. Then when the truth comes out, and it almost always does, we are forced to take responsibility for our actions.

In politics, there's an old adage that the coverup is always worse than the crime. I think that's true in everything. There will always be consequences for our actions, and those consequences will be worse if we're not honest from the start.

The whole experience of being caught in a lie and dealing with the consequences brings an element of grief to the guilty party. It's not the same level of grief you experience in dealing with a major tragedy or serious illness, but there is still a level of grief.

Counselors recognize the five phases of grief as denial, anger, bargaining, depression, and acceptance. I know that I have experienced that myself.

In my broken window experience, I went from:

1. Denial: "I can't believe I broke the window. That didn't really just happen, did it?" to

2. Anger, as I referenced myself in the second person: "You dummy, what were you thinking? You should not have been throwing the baseball in that direction, you idiot!" to

3. Bargaining: "How can I explain this to Mom and Dad? Who can I blame? What story can I put together that would exonerate me?" When bargaining with Dad failed and I was caught in the lie, I continued on to

4. Depression, as I faced the consequences of my actions: "Boy, am I in trouble. I wonder what kind of punishment I'll get from Dad for breaking the window and lying about it," and finally

5. Acceptance, knowing I got what was coming to me, then moving on: "Thank you sir, may I have another? I deserved that. By the way, Mom, what's for dinner?"

In my broken window experience, I wasn't grieving the loss of the window. It was more about grieving what would (and did) happen to me as a result.

As an adult, I can appreciate Dad's response. He must have been upset about the window and the cost to replace it, but he spoke not one word about it after I was disciplined for lying. After all, it wasn't about the broken window. It was about the way I handled it. It was about my honesty and integrity, or lack thereof.

My consequence for lying was swift and fair. I spent very little time being depressed over the whole thing and sailed right through to acceptance. Within a matter of days, the broken window was repaired. It took a lot more time than that to repair the broken trust my parents had in me. That was a valuable life lesson.

I wish I could say that I never told another lie after the broken window incident, but that would, in itself, be a lie. However, I can say that I chose to be honest on a much more regular basis from that point on.

Being honest may not always be the easiest choice, but I can say with absolute certainty that it is always the best choice. Like my parents, Benjamin Franklin, and many others before me, I have come to conclude that honesty and integrity are the greatest virtues.

Broken Norms

I have many fond memories of those early days in Idaho Falls, in the neighborhood surrounding Angels ballpark. My mind can easily drift back to those carefree times when Brice and I would explore the neighborhood and play pickup games of baseball and football for hours on end. I wouldn't trade those days for anything.

If I could go back and change *one thing*, it would be to embrace the Duttons with open arms right from the start. I wouldn't shun them myself, and I wouldn't tolerate them being shunned by any of the other kids in the neighborhood. I simply wouldn't stand by and allow that to happen. That would be a cause worth fighting for. I would gladly suffer a few more black eyes if that's what it took to effect a change.

It's amazing to me that a whole community could so readily ostracize one family for no apparent reason, other than the fact that that's what everyone else did. And it wasn't just the kids who were responsible. Any of the other parents could have stepped up and put an end to it. It went on for long enough that everyone had to know that it was happening.

I really don't think anyone can claim ignorance. The whole community shared in the blame, myself included. I didn't necessarily like being part of it, but I went along to get along. I gave in to peer pressure, and I became part of the problem. It took someone with a heart of compassion, someone like my mom, to recognize the wrong, and to step up and say something.

When we opened our baseball games to the Duttons, the walls of I don't know how many years of discrimination against them came crumbling down. That had to be liberating for them. I can't speak for others, but it certainly was liberating for me.

In my heart, I knew that not letting the Duttons play was wrong. And I didn't like having to make excuses to Eddie (or Mom) for not doing anything to change it. I'm pretty sure Brice felt the same way.

Mom ignited that spark of compassion in me and touched my heart for the Duttons. It made me want to do everything I could to change things for them. And when things finally did change, when the Duttons showed up to play, I felt a huge weight lifted off my shoulders. It was, well . . . liberating.

It didn't strike me so much at the time, but reflecting back on it, I think the day we let the Duttons play was one of the proudest moments of my life. Sure, Mom was a big part of it, steering us in the right direction, but we followed through and made it happen.

Brice and I played ball with Eddie and the Duttons for several years, from early grade school through junior high. During that time, we not only honed our skills and kept ourselves in shape, but we learned a valuable lesson in compassion.

That small act of kindness cost us nothing, but it gained us a true friendship, a friendship based on deep, mutual respect for each other. That level of respect and camaraderie only comes through weathering a storm together. In this story, it was Eddie and the Duttons who had endured the storm; Brice and I merely helped to see them through it.

The years have clouded my memory of those long–ago days, playing baseball at the Highland Park ball field and football in the outfield of Angels ballpark. I no longer remember the names and faces of most of the neighborhood kids who were part of our games, but I'll never forget Eddie, Joe, and Terry.

Though we have long since gone separate ways (pursuing girls and cars, pursuing educations and careers, raising families, and just doing life), they will always hold a special place in my heart. Whatever the game might be, Eddie and the Duttons can play on my team anytime!

EPILOGUE

D ad and Mom divorced when I was twelve. They still loved each other but could not live together. It was too much of a fight. They remarried about four years later, but that only lasted a few months. They just couldn't make it work. They both struggled with alcoholism, but where Dad was a mean drunk; Mom was a happy one.

Dad and Mom both died young from the effects of alcoholism: Dad at 52, Mom at 60. Somehow, those evils did not befall any of us kids. We all married once and have remained happily married to our first and only spouses. And none of us have struggled with alcohol or drug addictions. Whether that was a matter of witnessing our parents destroy their lives, providential, or just blind luck, who is to say? However you view it, we beat the odds.

Brett, true to form, got his first job in high school working as a projectionist at the local movie theater. After college, he ended up going to work in the aerospace industry for my company's competitor, where he worked for over thirty-six years. Brett enjoys target shooting and has a makeshift weapons training gallery in his basement "for the grandkids" (complete with ninja stars). He helped direct several plays for the youth at his church. On Halloween, Brett's house is the most decorated in his neighborhood. He is married with four children.

Brett, me, Dad, Brice, and Brenda, circa 1977
(Looking like a '70s rock band with their manager)

I followed in my dad's footsteps right after high school. I attended college at Idaho State University and went to work in the nuclear industry at the Idaho National Engineering Laboratory. After a few years, I left the nuclear industry and went to graduate school at the Georgia Institute of Technology. From there, I landed a job in the aerospace industry, where I retired after thirty-five years of service. I am married with three children.

Besides playing organized softball, I continued to play pickup games of football whenever I had a chance. Every Thanksgiving, I organized a friendly game of flag football with family and friends. I now enjoy watching my grandchildren play baseball (yes!), football (yes!), volley-ball, and soccer.

Brice spent most of his career in the pharmaceutical industry. He rode his bike to work almost every day for about twenty-five years, missing only two days due to inclement weather. This feat was heralded in the local town paper. Brice also coached his kids in soccer. He still plays Ultimate Frisbee with the mostly younger adults in his neighborhood. And he puts most of them to shame. Brice is married with three children.

Brenda married a sailor who trained with the nuclear navy at the Idaho National Engineering Laboratory. Her husband has worked in the computer technology business for over thirty years. Brenda worked a few sales jobs when she could, but she mostly stayed home to raise three children and one grandchild.

Joe Dutton served in the navy for eight years. He enlisted just prior to the end of the Vietnam War and served three years in the Philippines. Following his military service, Joe worked as a patrol officer, a service from which he retired after twenty-eight years. Joe is married with six children. He coached all of his kids in baseball, and he enjoys hiking with his wife.

Terry Dutton worked with the city sanitation department for over thirty years. He's married with three children. Besides spending time with family, Terry has enjoyed fishing, where he can get away and enjoy the outdoors.

Eddie Johnson was one of those who made a few bucks as a kid working in the Angels scoreboard box. As an adult he worked in the transportation industry for most of his career, drove buses for a number of different school districts, and ran his own transportation company for several years. Ed is married with three children. He's now retired and enjoys getting out on the golf course as often as he can.

Notes

1. Though attributed to Benjamin Franklin, these words were originally written by Sir Edwin Sandys, *Europae Speculum*, 1599.

2. Napoleon Hill and W. Clement Stone, *Success through a Positive Mental Attitude*, (New York: HarperCollins Publishers, 1997).

3. Desmond Tutu, *God Has a Dream: A Vision of Hope for Our Time*, (New York: Doubleday Religious Publishing Group, 2004).

4. *Hidden Keys to Loving Relationships - 05 How to Become Best Friends*, DVD, Gary Smalley, (Branson, MO: Smalley Relationship Center), 2005.

5. Robert Fulghum, *All I Really Need to Know I Learned in Kindergarten*, (New York: Villard Books, 1988).

6. The Coasters, "Charlie Brown," Atco Records, 1959.

7. Jim Croce, "You Don't Mess Around with Jim," track #1 on *You Don't Mess Around with Jim*, ABC Records, 1972, vinyl.

8. Yogi Berra, *The Yogi Book*, (New York: Workman Publishing, 1998).

9. John Wesley Powell, *Down the Colorado: Diary of the First Trip through the Grand Canyon*, 1869.

10. Berra, *The Yogi Book.*

11. Thomas Edison, unsourced, though often attributed to an interview for the *New York Times.*

12. Thomas Edison, *The Edison & Ford Quote Book*, (Carlisle, MA: Applewood Books, 2003).

13. Will Rogers and Joseph Carter, *Never Met a Man I didn't Like, (New York: William Morrow Paperbacks, 1991).*

14. Odell Beckham, Jr., interview by *ESPN* reporter Anita Marks, 2016.

15. Joseph Hincks, "Son Heung-min Wants to Bring World Cup Glory to South Korea," *Time*, June 7, 2018.

About the Author

Blake Murri is a retired nuclear engineer and rocket scientist who spent most of his career as an engineer/manager working for a major defense contractor in the Denver area. Immediately following retirement, Blake and his wife went to Okinawa, Japan, where they served as short-term missionaries to our men and women in uniform.

Blake is a long-serving member and elder in his church, where he regularly helps with facility maintenance. He's a member of his church's Master's Men, who do various projects for widows, single moms, and elderly in the community. For several years, Blake has led his church, in coordination with Habitat for Humanity and Help Build Hope, in a family-friendly project to build house frames in the church parking lot. Those frames are used for housing developments in lower–income neighborhoods in the Denver area.

Blake loves the outdoors, where he enjoys hunting, fishing, and hiking. He and his wife have three children and four grandchildren, with whom they spend as much time as possible.

CPSIA information can be obtained
at www.ICGtesting.com
Printed in the USA
BVHW040607060922
646102BV00007B/15

9 781955 043861